Love . . . and Death

LOVE . . .
and DEATH

Talks on
Contemporary
and
Perennial
Themes
by
Abraham Kaplan

Ann Arbor
The University of Michigan Press

Copyright © by Abraham Kaplan 1973
All rights reserved
ISBN 0-472-50465-7
Library of Congress Catalog Card No. 72-93402
Published in the United States of America by
The University of Michigan Press and simultaneously
in Don Mills, Canada, by Longman Canada Limited
Manufactured in the United States of America

*Acknowledgments are made to the following publishers and agents for permission to
use copyrighted materials:*

To Harcourt Brace Jovanovich, Inc., and Faber and Faber Ltd., for excerpts from T. S.
Eliot's *Collected Poems 1909-1962,* copyright, 1936, by Harcourt Brace Jovanovich,
Inc.; copyright © 1963, by T. S. Eliot. Reprinted by permission.

To Holt, Rinehart and Winston, Inc., and The Society of Authors as the literary
representative of the Estate of A. E. Housman, and Jonathan Cape Ltd., for "A
Shropshire Lad"—Authorized Edition—from *The Collected Poems of A. E. Housman.*
Copyright 1939, 1940, © 1965 by Holt, Rinehart and Winston, Inc. Copyright © 1967,
1968 by Robert E. Symons. Reprinted by permission.

To the Macmillan Company, for excerpts from Edwin Arlington Robinson's *Collected
Poems.* Copyright © 1921 by Edwin Arlington Robinson, renewed 1949 by Ruth
Nivison. Reprinted by permission.

To Helen Wax Cook
and the memory of Abraham Wax
for the love I have known
from them and theirs

Foreword

Educational television should have one resource that is not always available to commercial television—thoughtful, articulate people. Unfortunately, many American professors are thoughtful but not articulate and even more are articulate but not thoughtful. Abraham Kaplan is a delightful combination of both, and the television series "The Worlds of Abraham Kaplan" was one of the most sparkling, stimulating, and personal series we have ever produced.

That this series is now available in book form will be welcome news to Professor Kaplan's many admirers who have written to us from all parts of the nation asking for print versions of his talks. One great limitation of television is its absence of "think" time. You can't hold the TV picture in your lap, stop it, think over what was just said. The picture moves on. Now, with the publication of *Love . . . and Death: Talks on Contemporary and Perennial Themes* the reader can quite literally hold Professor Kaplan in his lap and ponder, agree, disagree. And there is much to ponder: Love, Women, Religion, Morals, Technology, Free Speech, Unreason, Loneliness, Mental Health, Aging, and Death.

Kaplan's interests range over all the deepest questions of traditional human experience. Armed with Shakespeare, the Bible, Plato, Maimonides, poets old and new, Kaplan leads us through the processes of his extremely individualistic mind and in so doing stimulates the reader to a newer awareness of his own individuality. With Abraham Kaplan, the reader is in the hands of a master teacher, a philosopher, a gadfly, and a delightful and impassioned storyteller.

For a television producer it was an exciting experience. My thanks to Professor Garnet R. Garrison, Director of Broadcasting, who let me convince him that one man, talking alone to a camera, without rehearsals, could hold a mass audience in this age of visual effects. My thanks to Professor Kaplan who showed once more that the greatest natural resource of educational television is always an intelligent and articulate human being.

Alfred Slote
Associate Director of the
University of Michigan Television Center

Preface

Education is always a cooperative venture, and on television especially so. In this venture I enjoyed the cooperation of the following crew:

Alfred Slote, *Producer*
Malcolm Campbell, *Production Director*
Marcia Domurat, *Associate Production Director*
Mike Freese, *Cameraman*
Jim Brian, *Cameraman*
Greg Appleton, *Cameraman*
Dick Hoesli, *Cameraman*
Norm Johnson, *Floor Manager*
Mary Phyl Godfroy, *Floor Assistant*
Tavi Fulkerson, *Floor Assistant*
Bob Burd, *Sound Engineer*
Mike Prestini, *Staging Designer*
Randy Brooks, *Staging Designer*

To all of them, my warm appreciation.

Abraham Kaplan
Haifa, Israel

Contents

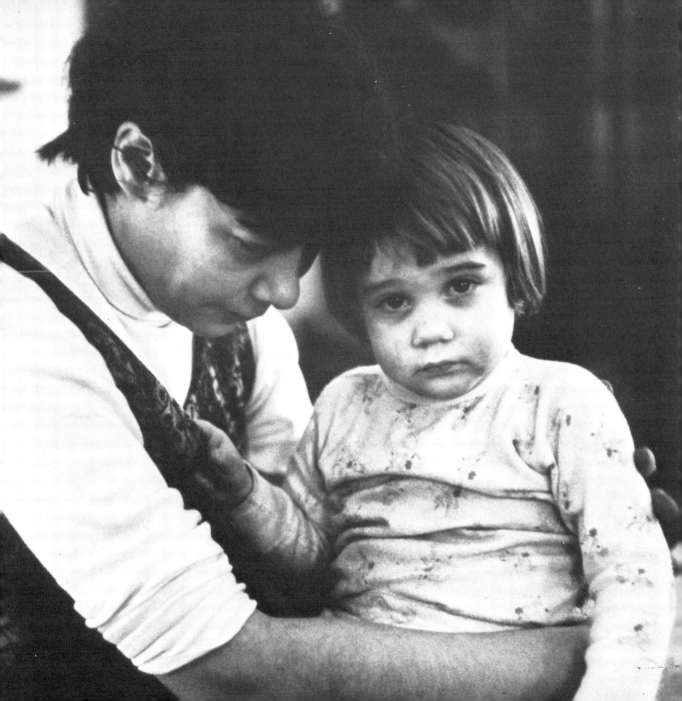

On Love

The most important elements of human experience are the most nearly universal. The problem is to be able to put words to them. I don't suppose that there is any man who does not know what love is. Yet to be able to articulate our knowledge is a skill for which we have to turn to the poets.

Shakespeare has formulated for all time the first of the fundamental components of love of which I want to speak:

> Let me not to the marriage of true minds
> Admit impediments. Love is not love
> Which alters when it alteration finds
> Or bends with the remover to remove.
> O, no! it is an ever fixed mark
> That looks on tempests and is never shaken;
> It is the star to every wand'ring bark,
> Whose worth's unknown, although his highth be taken.
> Love's not Time's fool, though rosy lips and cheeks
> Within his bending sickle's compass come.
> Love alters not with his brief hours and weeks,
> But bears it out even to the edge of doom.
>   If this be error, and upon me proved,
>   I never writ, nor no man ever loved.

Love is, first of all, a *commitment*. When we love, we are doing something more than responding with the particular feelings which we happen to have at the moment. Of all the factors of love, the element of commitment is the one that is least commonly acknowledged today. We are so much wrapped up in our own feelings of the particular moment. There is, in fact, a romantic myth of an *eternal moment* in which the significance of our whole past and our whole future is brought to a focus. There *is* something of that focusing in love, but only if we have committed ourselves. No matter how I happen to feel at any particular moment in the future, my

Commitment

love will still abide; it alters not, even when it alteration finds, whether in me or in you.

Caring   The commitment of love is to care, and *caring* is the second basic element in love. To love is not to be in a particular state of feeling; love is not something which is happening inside my heart, or anywhere inside me; love is something which is happening *between us*. It is a set of actions in which what matters to me is you; and what matters to me about you is not the kind of feeling that you can give to me, but your welfare. What matters to me is what you need and what you want.

Paralleling the romantic myth of the eternal moment which destroys commitment is another myth which destroys caring: the myth of *instant intimacy*. This myth proclaims it is a very easy thing to love. All that is necessary is for me to want to love and for you to be willing for me to love you. But what this myth overlooks is that if I am to care for you, if I am to meet your needs and your wants, I have to know what your needs are and what your wants are. And coming to know a person, whether myself or you, is an undertaking that goes far beyond the instant.

There is still another myth which interferes with caring. We often talk about caring as though it were transferring something from me to you. This implies that after I have given, I have less of something than I had before. But love is just the contrary: somehow, the more I give the more I have left. The myth of caring as giving implies that there was something in me to start with, then somehow it has been carried over and mysteriously infused into you. But what really comes to be is something which owes its existence to the fact of love between us. It was not already there to start with; it has no antecedent existence independent of the love relationship.

Caring is a certain kind of activity—an activity which, to be sure, expresses itself in a wide variety of ways, but an activity nevertheless. It is not the expression of a rootless feeling inside me, nor does it merely engender a correspondingly rootless feeling inside you, but, in an objective way it contributes to your growth and your fulfillment.

It is very easy for all of us to deceive ourselves into supposing that we are caring for another when in fact what we are doing is looking out for ourselves. We make certain demands on others, and we deceive ourselves into supposing that if only others meet our demands, we will be caring for them. But this is totally contrary to a third fundamental element of love, namely, *acceptance* of others. Love does not demand that you **Acceptance** meet my standards; it accepts you with your standards, and even with shortcomings from your standards (for all of us aspire to something more than we are). Love is the capacity to accept others as they are, as well as to accept their aspirations.

There is in love, I believe, a fundamental element of *respect*. **Respect** To say that I respect you is to say that I recognize your right to be the person who you are. And to say that I care for you is to say that I care for the person who you are. I think this is the substance of what the poets have described as being loved for oneself alone. Do not say you love me for this or for that: if love has its reasons, then when the reasons disappear so also will the love. I am not really loving, I am not really accepting, I am weighing and measuring you; and only if you are weighed and not found wanting, *then* I will . . . . But that is not love. What is especially tragic in human relations, and so often stands in the way of love, is the fact that the scale by which I weigh and measure you is all too often only a reflection of what I am in myself. We are both diminished by that measure.

Today in many ways, not only in relationships among individuals but also in relationships among groups, there is a widespread confusion between genuine *community*, which binds people together, and *identity*, sheer sameness. Parents very often demand of their children that they be, not the young men and women they are in themselves, but identical extensions, reflections, copies of what their parents are. In the same way, children often demand of parents that the parents be different people than *they* are. There is no real acceptance from either direction.

The gap between the generations is as universal a feature of human experience as is the experience of love. It seems to me to be futile, and pointless even if not futile, to try to bridge the gap, to overcome it, to deny it. What love means is that we are capable of reaching out across the gap. There is a myth here too, a myth connected with acceptance: it is the myth that love is blind—because when a person who does not love sees the faults in a person whom I love, he can only imagine that I love because I am blind to those faults. If he also loved this person, he too would accept him, faults and all. He certainly would not be blind to them. A young man comes to a father and says, "Sir, I would like to marry your daughter." The father answers, "Marry my daughter? You must be crazy! Have you ever seen her room, have you ever listened to her on the telephone, do you know what her closet is like, have you ever seen her in a kitchen?" The young man says, "Sir, I am perfectly well aware of her faults." And the father springs up with "Faults? What faults?"

Genuine love isn't blind to faults, but cherishes even the faults while accepting the aspirations of the beloved to free himself of them.

Sharing

Love, next, is a *sharing*. I commit myself to you, and that is something I do to you; and it may be that you also make a commitment to me. But at most what we have here is only a *reciprocity*. I care about you, and it may be that you care about me; that is also a reciprocal relationship. I accept you, you accept me, and that too is an exchange. Love goes beyond. In love there is something which we do together. There is more than a reciprocity; there is a *mutuality*. There is a sharing, and doing together things which neither of us could do without the other.

There is a romantic mythology of an unrequited love, as though love is something which can find a habitation within my own breast, quite regardless of where you are, what you are, and what we are doing with one another. There is no such thing as unrequited love; there may be a willingness to love, a readiness to love, a resource for loving—which is to say, there are human beings. But when we are alienated from one another, when we are in some way apart from one another, when we have not come to a sharing, then we may have a sense of unrequited love; but, in fact, what has happened is that love has not come to be at all.

In communication, which is putting into words what binds people together, there is a form which involves only a reciprocity. I call it "duologue." Two people are talking, but they are not really talking *with* one another, as would be the case in a genuine dialogue. When one of them is talking, the other one is supposedly listening; it may be that what he is actually doing is thinking of what he will say when it is his turn to talk. In any case there is no dialogue. Instead there is something which exists beforehand, a message or a content which is independent of the relationship. It is brought into the situation and then moved from one person to another.

That is often the pattern in other human relationships: we make *contracts* with one another. I will give you certain goods and services, provided that, in return, you will make certain payments to me. If the payments are not forthcoming, I may feel that I have been cheated—as parents may feel that their children are ungrateful, or a student may feel that the teacher has not given him the grade or the recognition that he deserves, or as in all sorts of human relationships we may feel that we are being taken advantage of.

In love there are no advantages to be taken. There is no contract to start with. But there is a *covenant*. There is something unconditional, something absolute involved in the commitment, in the caring, and in the sharing which belongs to real love.

I have said thus far that love involves commitment, caring, acceptance, and sharing. But how can we understand in these terms the measureless significance which love has had in human experience? Somehow, however important these characteristics may be in themselves, they seem rather colorless; or, at any rate, they have not yet brought into focus the passions, the excitement, the inchoate feelings for which we turn to music and poetry and song to find expression. In a word, if words are to be turned to, in love there is, finally, the element of *joy*.

Joy

These days we have become so very self-conscious about so many features of human experience that joy is in danger of being lost. We have come to a point where we are publishing advice and manuals on all the arts of living, but the very fact that the manuals are couched in terms of the technical competence which some people have, and expertise which the rest of us do not have, takes the life, spontaneity, and joy out of these human concerns. It is almost as though we can expect to find any day now someone publishing a little book with the title "Four Simple Steps to Spontaneity." Indeed, there are manuals in existence on how to play with your children, and countless sex manuals. I don't deny that there are matters of technical skill and competence in all areas of human existence. A man's nerves and muscles may be perfectly sound, and yet a golf pro might be able to tell him something about how to hit a golf ball. There are things which we all have yet to learn on how to live with children and parents, how to cultivate our minds or our various interests, and how to relate to one another as the human beings that we are. Yet a manual, not on sex but on how to love one another, would surely have to be a summation of all the world's wisdom. For in reality, to be capable of love is no less than to be capable of actualizing all our potentialities. For me to love is for me to be all that I am capable of being. I cannot love with anything less than my whole self, and in loving I cannot be less than all that I am capable of being in that act of love.

Here again the poets have said it better than anyone else, and I would like to turn to another poem of Shakespeare's, on how the experience of love can be fulfilling:

When, in disgrace with Fortune and men's eyes,
I all alone beweep my outcast state,
And trouble deaf heaven with my bootless cries,
And look upon myself and curse my fate,
Wishing me like to one more rich in hope,
Featur'd like him, like him with friends possess'd,
Desiring this man's art, and that man's scope,

With what I most enjoy contented least;
Yet in these thoughts myself almost despising,
Haply I think on thee, and then my state,
Like to the lark at break of day arising
From sullen earth, sings hymns at heaven's gate;
   For thy sweet love rememb'red such wealth brings
   That then I scorn to change my state with kings.

To love, to give and to receive love, is to be in such a state of fulfillment and joy that nothing external which can be provided for us by society, or by actions in which other human beings are not involved, can take its place.

There are many species of love in addition to the love between a man and a woman: the love of parents for children and of children for parents, the love of friends for one another, and a man's love for his country, his people, his profession, or his hobbies—everything that is his. For the self is fulfilled and enlarged precisely by this; when we love we reach out to the other and embrace him. The boundaries of the self are thereby enlarged. The other is brought in, is incorporated into myself, not by first being made over into my image, but as the person *he* is. When we love, neither of us is quite the person that he was before. Both of us are transformed by love. Both of us have grown; in that growth the self finds its fulfillment.

Growth   It is because of these experiences of *growth,* of loyalty and commitment, of love, of caring for something and someone else, of acceptance, and of taking others for what they are and sharing with them that totalitarian societies in all times and places have been so hostile to love. Those who set out to destroy men's minds and to control their lives, to make of other men only the materials for their own ends, put themselves in the place of God, making men over into their image, but with this difference: that where we have been, in fact, endowed by God with a great and boundless capacity for love, in the totalitarian societies it is precisely that capacity, above all others, which is denied to us. This was eloquently commented on by the ancient philosopher Plato, who knew that autocrats always deny the capacity for love and who remarked in his great dialogue on love, "If there were only some way of contriving that a State, or an army, should be made up of lovers, they would be the very best governors," better even than the philosophers who Plato thought should rule the ideal State. "And," he said, "when fighting at each other's side, although a mere handful, the lovers would overcome the world."

On Women

There is, I suppose, a certain presumption in a man venturing to talk about the psychology of women. In a sense, it is true that no man can really know women; yet men can read, and men think about women all the time. Even in terms of my personal qualifications, it has sometimes seemed to me that I have spent a very large part of my life in the company of women, since I had been raised by my mother, together with six sisters and only one brother, and I am married and have two daughters. Still I think these personal qualifications should be irrelevant.

There is very much at work today a certain assumption about what a man needs in order to have knowledge. I call it the *axiom of direct experience*. According to this axiom, if a man has direct experience of a certain subject matter, he knows whatever is to be known about it; and if he does not have that direct experience, he cannot lay claim to knowledge. But if that axiom were true, we would have to admit that every one of the 800 million Chinese is an expert on China and every phase of Chinese life or, for that matter, that every one of the 200 million Americans can lay claim to expertise about American life. This is obviously not the case. To insist on direct experience as a basis of knowledge is to deny what is essentially human. For the human being is the only animal which can learn without direct experience. Only humans can learn from the experience of others of our species. If men are ever to learn anything at all about women, it will not be by direct experience but by observation, by reflection on what we observe, and by opening our minds—and perhaps our hearts also—to what women have to tell us about their own direct experience.

It takes very little observation and very little reflection to

Direct Experience

Discrimination

recognize that the greatest problem which confronts women in the modern world is fundamentally the problem of *discrimination*. Discrimination is not a simple matter to explain, because in a sense all education aims at cultivating our powers of discrimination. To be able to discriminate means only to respond to different stimuli in different ways. But the kind of discrimination which makes a problem for women, blacks, Catholics, Jews, Chicanos, and all sorts of minorities and special groups in our society is this: they are responded to differently in situations in which the differences make no difference. They are discriminated against because certain *irrelevant* factors are being introduced. For example, on the average, women in the United States earn only about two-thirds as much pay as men for doing the same work. The only relevant factor in the determination of pay, it seems to me, is the work that is done. If a woman does as much and does as well as a man, I cannot see any justification for not paying her the same wage as a man would earn. That is the discrimination from which women have suffered, and continue to suffer in our society.

Prejudice

Women are also victimized in another way—by *prejudice*—by having feelings directed toward them and being thought about in ways which depend, not upon the real characteristics of the particular individual woman, but upon certain preconceptions about women which our predominantly male-dominated culture provides. When Adam sinned in the Garden of Eden and God called him to account, he said, as has been the way of men ever since, "The woman gave it to me, and I did eat thereof." Adam, in fact, was not content with blaming the woman; he also shifted the responsibility onto God: "The woman that You provided me with gave it to me." He was passing the buck doubly.

Everyone knows that Helen of Troy destroyed both Greek and Trojan, Cleopatra cost Marc Antony a world, and Delilah cost Samson his strength and ultimately his life. There are many places in our culture, even in Scripture, where we are warned against the wiles of women. The Preacher says, "I found more bitter than death the woman whose heart is snares and nets, and whose hands are fetters. A man who pleases God may escape her, but the sinner is taken by her." "Behold, this is what I found," says the Preacher, "adding one thing to another, my mind has sought repeatedly but I have not found; one man among a thousand I found, but a woman among all these I have not found." Men have been warned throughout history and from earliest youth against the wiles of women. Some philosophers, notably pessimists like Schopenhauer, have even expressed wonder that anybody should ever be tempted by this creature. Schopenhauer says in a famous, or infamous, essay on women: "It is only the man whose intellect is clouded by his sexual impulses that could give the name of 'the fair sex' to that under-sized, narrow-shouldered, broad-hipped, and short-legged race."

Very characteristically prejudices quite often run in two different directions. Frequently our attitudes are, as the psychologists say, *ambivalent;* we exaggerate certain desirable qualities, as though in this fashion we can compensate for our exaggeration of the undesirable ones. Thus, we also have the stereotypes of women as the creative and protective mother; of woman as the inspiration, the eternal feminine which draws us ever onward and upward; of woman as the keeper of moral and aesthetic values, without whom man would sink into brutishness. The extraordinary thing is that these prejudicial stereotypes of snare and inspiration exist side by side. Together, they can serve to rationalize and maintain a vicious system of social discrimination.

In these perspectives it is very understandable that many women today feel that it is high time to repudiate the patterns in which women are relegated to a subordinate position in society. Unfortunately, some groups which present themselves as aiming at the liberation of women have pictured man as an enemy. Apparently working on the supposition that two wrongs will make a right, they have proclaimed that prejudices against women are to be countered by prejudices against men, as though discriminations against women will somehow be equalized if there are corresponding discriminations against men. They view the relationship between men and women as a state of continued belligerency, and have set for themselves the task of serving as terrorists and guerrilla fighters in that cold war.

I believe that the fundamental mistake which is made most often in groups that aim at the liberation of women is this: *instead of demanding that we change our ways of treating women, they have insisted that women should be treated just like men.* Thus they have attempted to deny the differences between men and women. I must emphasize again, not only in connection with this pattern of discrimination but in connection with so many of the discriminations in our society, that what counts is not a denial of differences, but our capacity to recognize differences for what they are, and even to prize and cherish them.

Many people talk nowadays about the problems which women face in trying to determine their identity. There is something of a *crisis* of identity for many people in our time: for the young, for the old, and for members of various minori-

Crisis of Identity

ty groups. The problem of identity for women has been made particularly severe because of the perpetuation of a certain romanticist illusion about the nature of women and their part in society, an illusion which was very clearly formulated by Lord Byron in the last century in his *Don Juan:* "Man's love," he says, "is of man's life a thing apart, 'tis woman's whole existence." This conception, which is so familiar to all of us, does a grave injustice to both men and women: it denies to women an opportunity for productive work, and it denies to men a channel for the expression of their own deep emotional needs.

For women particularly, it seems to me, there has been a problem in the recognition of certain components of the human personality which are as important in the personality of women as in the personality of men, but which our society has seen as somehow not consistent with our stereotypes of femininity. I mean the element of *aggression,* of determination, of strength, the capacity to move toward a goal in the face of obstacles. This is a capacity which is characteristic of all living organisms. Life itself is an unending succession of problems with which we must cope so that even if we cannot solve them, we can, at any rate, move onward to the next problems. **Aggression**

Every woman knows very well the tremendous demands which are made upon her strength, upon all her resources, to cope with the problems which confront her every hour of every day. But in our stereotypes, femininity is equated with a certain kind of *passivity,* with a certain kind of yieldingness, with a certain incapacity to bring energies to bear on external difficulties. Think of all the various nicknames which we apply to women: bunny, chick, bird, mouse, pigeon, and pussycat; all soft and gentle little things. Yet, ironically, we men also de- **Passivity** mand of a woman that she have a great deal of strength when we want to lean upon her. We assign to women many different roles which are by no means always compatible with one another. The crisis of identity for women in our time is, I think, to a very significant degree, a crisis produced by *role conflicts.* At times a woman does not know exactly what she is expected to be, and even when she does know, often she finds that these expectations interfere with other demands which are also being made upon her.

Male Identity

It should be pointed out that this *identity* crisis is something that is experienced by men as well, and for reasons which are closely connected with those operative in the crisis of female identity. The human animal differs from other animals in his capacity to learn and to share in the experience of others of his species. We have also another capacity. We can conceal our feelings and even misrepresent them. If the dog wags his tail, he's happy; and if he's happy, he wags his tail. It is not so with human beings. A man may smile and smile but be a villain. In this regard women, if I may say so, are even more human than men. Women have a greater capacity than men to conceal, and perhaps misrepresent, their feelings. In the crudest biological terms, a man cannot conceal his state of sexual readiness, nor can he pretend to a state of sexual excitement which he does not really feel. This is not true for women. Something of the mystery which men have always seen in women (that inscrutable smile on the face of the Mona Lisa) may have its roots in the sense that the man has of not knowing exactly where the woman stands, especially in relationship to him. Every man experiences, at some point and to some degree, anxiety as to whether his inadequacies might not be exposed beyond any possibility of concealment or pretense.

Perhaps even more fundamentally, there is a crisis of male identity which points to something that is central biologically, psychologically, and culturally for women also. It is that women have the capacity to produce children. While it is true as a matter of strict genetics that a man contributes to the offspring exactly as many chromosomes as does the woman, the experience of childbirth, of nurturing the unborn infant and caring for it through its infancy, is much more of an intimate and significant experience for the woman than for the man. I have long felt that there must be operative in men something which we might call *uterus envy:* an envy of woman's capacity to create and to produce. Perhaps it is this envy that, at least in part, motivates men to build bridges and cities and to reach for the stars. Even in these awesome accomplishments man must make do with something second-best. Only a woman can give birth to children and can find a fulfillment in that possibility.

But it would certainly perpetuate existing discriminations if one were to say that because women have this capacity they do not have other capacities. Women may also be capable of building bridges and cities, as men are also capable of tender care, protection, and nourishment of the young, the weak, and the helpless. In fact, this tenderness must surely be central in the experiences of love which mature men and women have for one another. Too often love is stifled and kept immature because one party plays the part of the parent and the other assumes the role of the child. Very often the sexual component of the relationship serves as a *substitute* for love, and perhaps even as a *defense* against love, as both men and women feel that the challenge of giving themselves wholly to another human being is more than they are prepared to meet.

I believe the greatest injustice which our society has

perpetrated upon both women and men is that we have devoted so much of our resource to packaging women. We call it *glamour*. We have devoted ourselves to glamourizing the female form. There have been in all cultures and at all times an interest in and a responsiveness to the beauty of the human body. But what might have been a means to another end, what might have served as a way to enhance a human relationship has, alas, often taken the place of the real values which human beings can find in one another. There is, I think, a remarkable realism and a remarkable contemporary relevance in a love poem of William Shakespeare's, written some centuries ago:

> My mistress' eyes are nothing like the sun;
> Coral is far more red than her lips' red;
> If snow be white, why then her breasts are dun;
> If hairs be wires, black wires grow on her head.
> I have seen roses damask'd, red and white,
> But no such roses see I in her cheeks;
> And in some perfumes is there more delight
> Than in the breath that from my mistress reeks.
> I love to hear her speak; yet well I know
> That music hath a far more pleasing sound.
> I grant I never saw a goddess go:
> My mistress, when she walks, treads on the ground.
>   And yet, by heaven, I think my love as rare
>   As any she belied with false compare.

What is most deserving of love is not the glamourous image, but the real person, the real woman. But to be able to find joy in a relationship with a real woman, one would have to be also a real man.

On Religion

There are few areas of human concern which have played a more significant role in the history of the human species than religion. There are also few areas of human concern which are so much characterized, as is religion, by ignorance and prejudice, and by a certain very human blindness to points of view other than our own. For so many of us, what we know about religion is no more than what we have learned as children, or perhaps in a few years in our youth in Sunday schools. It is not surprising that we think of religion as childish, for it is only a childish religion with which we are acquainted. On the other hand, many whose knowledge of religion is much deeper tend to identify all religion, at all times and places in human culture, with the particular forms of religion with which they themselves are acquainted.

Ours is a time in which religion is undergoing revolutionary changes in many directions: changes in the structure of authority, changes in the human content of religious life and practice, changes in ritual, and changes in every dimension of the religious experience. At just such a time as this, many people view religion only through their own prejudices, and others approach the subject only as apologists for their own particular religious identity.

If we look at religion in the broadest human terms, I think what we see first, as essential to all religion, is a *church*. Every religion is first of all a community of the faithful. The word 'religion', in fact, derives from an expression meaning 'to bind together', and whatever other content that expression has, religion is one of those devices by which human beings are bound together into a community. Sometimes people express themselves as quite sympathetic to the religious life, and critical only of what they call "organized religion," without

Church

realizing that *the only alternative to organized religion is disorganized religion.* There has not been anywhere, at any time in human society, or to any significant degree, any religion which was not in this sense organized. History verifies that when human beings have important values to pursue, the form of their pursuit becomes institutionalized.

It is in the very nature of institutions not only to serve the values of their members, but also to serve their own interests. It is not rare that institutional concerns interfere with the primary values for which the institution was founded. There is no doubt that the church, as such, has sometimes interfered with religious life, just as there is no doubt that the university has sometimes interfered with education. Every human institution must recurrently be brought into closer harmony with the values which it is intended to serve.

It is ironic that although we all find shortcomings in government, we are not very inclined to become anarchists. Instead, we recognize that governments must continuously be made responsible to the interests of the governed. In the same way, though churches may have their shortcomings, this does not in itself provide any rational basis for repudiating their role in religion. It should serve, rather, as an incentive to bring the church into closer accord with the concerns of religion.

A religion, then, unifies certain groups of people, and it also sets them apart from other groups. In our time many people have approached religion from this standpoint: they have asked, "Can we not find some universal content in all religion so that we will have only one church and all be members of the same community of the faithful?" It seems to me that this kind of *universalism* is as empty an ideal as is the other ideal of our time, a universal language. There will not be a universal language until there is a universal human community. Religion, like language, has its roots very deep in the experience both of the individual and of his culture. Too often what we think of as an aspiration toward universality is only a way of reducing everyone else to our own level.

A story is told about an American under-secretary of state in the United Nations who said to a colleague, "Why can't Israel and her Arab neighbors settle their differences like Christian gentlemen?" To which a Buddhist, who overheard his remark, rejoined, "The trouble is, I'm afraid, that that's just what they are doing."

Creed

The story is apocryphal, of course. What is real and important is this very human tendency to suppose that what I believe must serve as a standard for all other human beings. It is this, I think, that is responsible for the divisiveness which so often characterizes religion. Because, in addition to being a church, every religion is also a *creed,* a set of beliefs. It is extraordinary what variety we can find in these beliefs. It is even more extraordinary that because of this variety, we find men set one against the other in the name of religion. Alas, quite often in human history seas of blood were spilled in the determination on the part of believers to impose their creed on their fellow men—by fire and the sword, if need be.

It seems to me that on this point philosophy has a particular contribution to make to the religious life. In one of Plato's dialogues Socrates is discussing certain conceptions of the gods and of their relationship to the universe. He concludes his discussion with these words: "If amid the many opinions about the gods and the origin of the universe, we are not able in every respect to make all our ideas consistent with each other and precisely accurate, no one need be surprised.

Enough if we are able to give an account which is no less likely than any other; for we must remember that I who speak, and you who judge of what I say, are only human beings, so that on these subjects we should be satisfied with a likely story and demand nothing more." Something of this intellectual humility, I think, is an important component of every truly viable religious creed.

It is often said that the creeds to be found in religion turn men's minds away from this world and its problems into some fantasy world, or at any rate, into some transcendent realm of being about which, in the very nature of the case, no one can claim to know with any certitude. Yet, over and over, in all of the world's major religions we find that the creed does not turn us away from the world, but, on the contrary, it brings us to a closer awareness and a fuller appreciation of this world.

In our Scripture, after the creation God Himself saw that the world was good. For man to declare that the world is in essence somehow evil, or to think that religion demands that we somehow turn our back upon the world, is to take a view which is not justified by the traditional creeds in any of the major religions. Although miracles play a part in many creeds, for many of them miracles constitute, not an exception to the natural order, but rather what is awesome and wonderful in nature itself. In this vein men like Einstein and Spinoza—in fact, scientists, philosophers, and thinkers of many ages and cultures—have found a religious faith sustained precisely by the enterprise of discovering order, law, and regularity in nature rather than by trying to find places in which something outside nature intervenes and upsets an established order. Such men, like the Psalmist, believe that the heavens declare the glory of God, and the firmament shows His handiwork.

In all religions the creed has an important and often essential component: a *moral doctrine*. We find the Golden Rule, for example, playing a part equally for Hillel, in ancient Judaism, for Confucius, for Jesus, and we find something very much like it also in Islam and in Hinduism. Similarly, peace and brotherhood are operative ideals in all major religions. In the Judaic Talmud, there is a question raised—indeed, it is the question with which the Talmud begins—as to the time of day when a man is permitted to recite his morning prayers. Does the morning begin on the stroke of midnight, or with the first flush of dawn, or only when the sun is high in the heavens? Among the replies given, one of the most significant is that which declares it is time to recite morning prayers when there is enough light for a man to recognize his brother. As long as we are still in such darkness that we do not recognize our brothers, it is not yet time for us to pray.

Cult   In addition to a church and a creed, every religion is also a *cult:* it is a set of practices, gestures, sacred objects, special occasions, and special circumstances. Its various symbols must be manipulated in accord with the requirements of the particular cult. We all know the dangers to the religious life which derive from this dimension of religion; namely, religious symbols can degenerate into a kind of empty ritualism, as though the symbol itself contains the reality of the religious life. This is a danger which has been well known to the great religious teachers in all cultures. It is the danger against which the prophet Isaiah thundered when he said in the name of God, "What to Me is the multitude of your sacrifices? I have had enough of your burnt offerings." Even though you recite many prayers, I will not listen; your hands are full of blood. "Wash yourselves, make yourselves clean, remove the evil of your deeds from before My eyes, cease to do evil and learn to do good. Seek justice, correct oppression, defend the fatherless, plead for the widow," and then, "though your sins be as scarlet, they shall become white as snow; though they are red like crimson, they shall become as wool." The prophet Amos spoke with similar vehemence: "I hate, I despise your feasts, I take no delight in your solemn assemblies; even though you offer Me your burnt offerings, I will not accept them, I will not look upon them. Take away from Me the noise of your songs; to the melody of your harps I will not listen; but, let justice roll down like the waters and righteousness like a mighty stream."

Ritual and symbolism have had a part to play in all religions; yet all religions recognize that what is most essential to the religious experience is moral action, and the worship of the heart. There is a beautiful story told by Anatole France (though it is a folk story, and many versions are known in many cultures) of a juggler who joins a monastery. A simple un-schooled man, he does not know the prayers and cannot share in the ritual service of his fellow monks. But in the middle of the night he comes down to the chapel, and before the statue of the Virgin Mary he stands on his head and performs his juggling act. The statue looks down upon him and smiles. Each man can serve only with what he has.

Religion is not only creed, not only church, not only cult; religion is also *faith*. This element of faith probably has been subject to more misunderstanding than any other element of the religious life. Many people have supposed that religious faith means that their religion can be used by them as a crutch, a cure-all, a way of healing physical illness, becoming suc-cessful in one's work, or coping with human relations in

Faith

the family, on the job, or elsewhere. But authentic religious life in all cultures and all faiths is something that comes out of the fullness of a man's heart. It is a gift in which we express our love, rather than something which comes out of the poverty of our lives as a demand that something be given to us.

All religion, no doubt, is rooted in the dark night of the soul, in which a man must wrestle with his angel against the doubts and despair into which we are plunged by a sense of our mortality, by a sense of our alienation from the world, and by a sense of our finitude, our limitations. In all of the major religions, faith has not meant a capacity to believe propositions without evidence, or in the face of the evidence; faith has not had to do with evidence. It has meant, rather, a capacity to commit ourselves, to entrust ourselves, to affirm the meaning and value of life, whatever the problems with which we are beset. What is fundamental in faith is an attitude of *humility,* of knowing our limitations as human beings, and an attitude of appreciation of life, affirmation of life, *gratitude* for life.

These two points of view, humility and gratitude, are most eloquently expressed in Scripture. When God answers Job out of the whirlwind with the question, "Who is this who darkens counsel by words without knowledge? Gird up your loins like a man, I will question you and you declare to Me: where were you when I laid the foundations of the earth? Tell Me if you have understanding. Who determined its measures, if you know? Who stretched the line upon it? On what were its bases sunk, or who laid the cornerstone, when the morning stars sang together, and all the sons of God shouted for joy?" It is good for a man to ask himself these questions whenever he experiences the temptation to mistake himself for a god, and to suppose that he has the right to determine how other human beings shall live.

The gratitude which is central to religious experience is beautifully exemplified in a very ancient Hebrew poem, the conclusion of which runs: "To You alone, O God, we give thanks; though our mouths were as full of song as the sea, though our tongues were as multitudinous as the waves and our lips of praise were as wide as the skies, though our eyes shone with light as the sun and the moon, though our hands were outspread as the eagles of heaven, though our feet were swift as the deer: even then, we would still be unable to thank You, O God, our God and the God of our fathers, for one thousandth or one ten-thousandth part of what You have done for our fathers and for us. Therefore, the limbs which You have fashioned, the spirit which You have breathed into our nostrils, the tongue which You have set in our mouths, all these shall thank You, bless You, praise You, You, always You, only You. Whatever in me is high shall be made humble, whatever is brave shall be in awe, whatever is glad shall be grateful; and every part of my being shall sing Ha-lelu Yah: praised be God."

Religion can be a matter of dependencies, but it can also be a matter of humility. It can express anxiety, but also trust. It can manifest guilt, but also moral responsibility. It can invite a life of fantasy, but it can also bring to a focus and provide a channel for expression of our joy in God's world.

On Morals

Many people have been talking about a sexual revolution in our time, or at any rate about some great change in the moral standards of our time. It is my impression, confirmed also by whatever I have been able to read about the subject, that this notion of some radical change in the behavior of the young, or of the rest of us, with regard to moral questions is really a mistaken one. There has been a change, to be sure, but not in our standards. The change has been in the *honesty* with which we profess standards that correspond to our behavior.

I have felt that for some time American morality could be described as a tyranny tempered only by hypocrisy. If there has been a rebellion, I think it has been more a rebellion against hypocrisy than against the standards which we all profess as governing our behavior. There is a story of a young instructor who was found in what used to be called a compromising situation with a lady not his wife. When he was called in to the dean and given a severe talking-to, he said, "Well, I was only found doing what everyone else around here does behind closed doors." The dean replied, "Young man, that's what doors are for."

That story, if not altogether a matter of folklore, certainly belongs to the morality of another time. If there has been a revolution in morals, it has centered around the insistence that what we do behind closed doors must meet the same standards of moral value as apply to our behavior elsewhere.

It seems to me that the first feature of the moral life in our time is *honesty*. There is a saying by one of the rabbis that the distance between the mouth and the heart is as great as the distance between heaven and earth. And yet, he added, the earth is nourished by rain from heaven. Morality is not only a matter of what we say. But what we say is not altogether irrele-

Honesty

29

vant if it corresponds to a commitment which we are prepared to make for action in terms of what we say.

Many of us, I believe, are engaged today in what could be called a *moral ventriloquism*. We make moral pronouncements and pretend that it is not we ourselves who are speaking, but that we are speaking on behalf of all Americans, or on behalf of our generation, or on behalf of all peace-lovers, or on behalf of one group or another. But as individuals we are reluctant to assume responsibility, as the particular human beings that we are, for the moral standards that we individually profess.

Openness

I think that the moral revolution in our time, if there has been one, involves not only honesty, but also *openness,* a recognition that moral standards are not all that easy to come by, and moral issues are not all that easy to resolve. There is a passage in Bernard Shaw's play *Major Barbara* in which the old munitions maker is talking with his twenty-four-year-old son about a possible career. Undershaft asks if he's interested in literature and the young man says, "No, I have nothing of the artist about me." Maybe philosophy? and he replies, "Oh, I make no such ridiculous pretension." Then Undershaft asks him about the army, the church, and the bar. The young man isn't interested in or knowledgeable about religion, or military affairs, or law, or any other such career. At last Undershaft asks, "Well come, is there anything you know or care for?" The son replies, "I know the difference between right and wrong." Undershaft retorts, "You don't say so. What, no capacity for business, no knowledge of law, no sympathy with art, no pretension to philosophy, only a simple knowledge of the secret that has puzzled all the philosophers, baffled all the lawyers, muddled all the men of business, and ruined most of the artists. The secret of right and wrong—why, man, you're a genius, a master of masters, a god—at twenty-four, too."

I think there is an increasingly widespread recognition in our time that the difference between right and wrong is not so easily known, not so easily come by. A French philosopher of the seventeenth century, sometimes called the father of modern philosophy, René Descartes, once observed that of all good things in the world, the one that is most fairly distributed is good sense, because every man is satisfied with his own share. But when it comes to distinguishing between right and wrong, we must turn not only to our own share of good sense, but also to the good sense claimed by others. Although many people in our time profess to clear-cut moral principles, the clarity of moral principle is often undermined, alas, by the ambiguities of moral practice. Many people pursue what might be noble ends, morally speaking, if only those ends could be isolated from the means which are employed to pursue them. But for the attainment of those ends, they employ means that in the eyes of others are seen to be the depths of immorality. We have witnessed, and continue to witness, the most outrageous inhumanities committed in the name of humanity.

A fundamental feature of the moral life, therefore, is to be open to the possibilities of error and of learning. This means, more specifically, to recognize an underlying *pluralism* in the **Pluralism** moral life, to recognize that there is a whole domain of values. In the house of the Lord there are many mansions, not only the particular one that I happen to be occupying. Bernard Shaw, in another of his plays, *Man and Superman,* has one of the characters, John Tanner, write a revolutionist's handbook. One of the maxims in this handbook is: "Don't do unto others as you would have them do unto you; their tastes may be different from yours." In our time there has been an increasing recognition, not merely that there are differences in tastes, but also that there are differences in actions even though the same high moral standard might be adhered to by the various actors. They may be acting in different situations, different contexts.

For a long time, since Aristotle at least, theorists have recognized that circumstances alter cases. This is true not only from a narrowly legal standpoint, but also from a moral standpoint. In particular, in a time like ours in which people of the most diverse cultural and ethnic backgrounds are thrust upon one another and in which we all recognize our common lot, it is more important than ever to recognize a fundamental difference between morals and ethics. The ways people act, or the ways they feel they should act, and the standards they pursue that to a greater or lesser degree actually guide their lives are part of the area of *morals*. On the other hand, the justifications people give for their particular standards and the theories that they adduce, whether from philosophy, religion, or experience, in order to present their morals in the best possible light fall under the domain of *ethics*.

We are coming more and more to appreciate that people may share the same morality even though they have very different ethics. People may agree that a certain measure should be adopted and should control or guide the lives of men, although one group of people may think this should be done because it will produce the greatest happiness for the greatest number, and another group of people may think it should be done because it is for the greater glory of God. If we demand that everyone share our own ethical theory, it is inevitable that we will lose the moral accord which we might otherwise realistically hope to attain.

It should also be recognized that people can agree in their ethical theory and still have sharp and destructive disagreements in concrete morality. We know this from the history of religious warfare and the great amount of blood that has been spilled by those who thought they were doing God's work and who saw in their enemies only the agents of the devil.

Among the ethical theories which I think are coming to play an increasingly significant part in contemporary morality are those that see moral standards as grounded fundamentally in man's nature. This point of view is classically called the position of *humanism,* provided we do not interpret that word in some narrow doctrinal sense, as though it is intrinsically antagonistic to religion or to other conceptions of the nature of man. Whatever the conception of man might be in its specifics, humanism teaches that the difference between right and wrong, good and bad, depends on what man is like, what manner of creature he is, and what will provide him not merely with momentary experiences of satisfaction, but with fulfillments of his potentialities.

Humanism

This, in the broadest terms, was the position taken by Aristotle; it was the position of the Stoics in the ancient world; it was the position of such later philosophers as Spinoza, as John Dewey in our own day; and the position of such philosophical psychologists as Sigmund Freud or our contemporaries Erich Fromm and Rollo May. For all these thinkers morality is not something which runs counter to man's nature—as though the natural man wishes to do evil, so that we must somehow make sure that instead he moves toward the good. On the contrary, for all of them the realization of moral value is indistinguishable from the fulfillment of man's own nature. In my own judgment, this is decidedly the position also of the great Judeo-Christian tradition of the Western world and indeed, the position of the major Asian religions as well. What is in man's nature, what fulfills man's nature, is work and love, or the combination of them in what we know as creation. It is precisely in these creative aspects of his life that man actualizes the elements of the Divine in whose image, in our tradition, he was created.

This is why the Book of Deuteronomy, in promulgating the moral law, emphasizes that moral standards do not have some mysterious and transcendent locus. "The Law which I teach you this day," the Deuteronomist declares, "is not hidden from you. It is not far off. It is not up in the sky that you should say, 'Who will go up to the sky and bring it down to us that we may hear it and obey it?' Nor is it beyond the sea, that you should say, 'Who will cross the sea and bring it back to us?' The word of God is very near to you. It is in your own mouth and in your heart." The word of God—that is to say, the standards of morality—are as close to us as is the very self.

Self-respect   The foundation of moral behavior lies in acceptance of the self—love of the self, if you will—it lies in *self-respect*. The man who has no respect for himself cannot have respect for others. If we are enjoined to love the other as we love ourselves, it is no good to say, "Well, I follow the Biblical injunction; it is true that I hate my neighbor, but I hate myself too." The injunction requires that we accept ourselves as the human beings that we are, with our frailties and shortcomings, and still, for all that, as created in the image of God—that is to say, as the locus of measureless value.

For young people maturing into responsible moral agents, the problems of morality tend to present themselves as problems of somehow accommodating our *desires* to our *duties.* I suppose that this accommodation can be regarded as a mark of coming to moral maturity. It was so formulated by the great philosopher of China, Confucius, who described his own moral development as culminating in a conquest of the opposition between duty and desire: "At fifteen," Confucius said of himself, "I thought only of study. At thirty, I began playing my role in life. At forty, I was sure of myself. At fifty, I was conscious of my position in the universe. At sixty, I was no longer a rebel. And now, at seventy, I can follow my heart's desire without violating what is right." If it took even Confucius a lifetime to bring duty and desire into consonance with one another, it is not to be wondered at that the attainment of moral maturity is still a central problem for most of us.

The modern temper emphasizes that to deal with this problem what is needed more than ever before in human history is an understanding of man and his nature, an understanding of society, an understanding of our relationship to the large world around us. In a word, what is needed is *knowledge.* Morality is not a matter simply of intentions. It is **Knowledge** true that in our tradition man's suffering began with his tasting the fruit of the tree of knowledge of good and evil. Yet I have often thought that the Fall consisted not so much in merely tasting of that fruit, but in the circumstance that man had so little of it. Even today we know so very much less than we need to know about ourselves as individuals, about our fellow man, about society, about mankind, about this world we live in. We know so very much less than we need to know in order to give to our moral aspirations a concrete basis with some realistic hope of coming close to our ideals.

I believe that a generation or two ago there was a widespread confusion of *virtue* and *innocence;* a confusion which is still expressed in our day, for example, in the widespread opposition and even hostility to sex education. We used to say, "Be good, fair maid, and let who will be clever." Today we recognize that it takes a good deal of cleverness to be good. We must have knowledge in order to be able to face the problems of attaining and maintaining peace and freedom, the problems of so disposing of our fantastic technology as to allow for the release of human potential instead of dehumanizing ourselves. The crucial moral problems which confront us on every side, issues such as abortion, euthanasia, population control, the pollution of our environment, all make demands upon our knowledge to the fullest reach of the human mind.

Morality in the past has often been trivialized. It has been made a matter of whether a man should be allowed to drink a glass of beer on Sunday, or whether a young woman should be allowed to wear her skirt this many or that many inches above or below the knee. But we know now that we cannot identify the good with what is merely goody-goody. Too often, I think, we have judged, especially with regard to our young people, that they were good when we meant only that they were not making trouble. But the great moral leaders of mankind, the prophets, the teachers, the martyrs—they have been the very men and women who made trouble. They made trouble because they saw that the people around them were leading troubled lives, and because they were passionately commited to the faith that it is possible for man to lead a life of greater fulfillment than that afforded by society or reached for by a majority.

A few generations ago, the English poet Matthew Arnold wrote a poem called "Dover Beach," the conclusion of which, alas, seems to have even more point and poignancy in our time than it did in his:

Ah, love, let us be true
To one another! for the world, which seems
To lie before us like a land of dreams,
So various, so beautiful, so new,
Hath really neither joy, nor love, nor light,
Nor certitude, nor peace, nor help for pain;
And we are here as on a darkling plain
Swept with confused alarms of struggle and flight,
Where ignorant armies clash by night.

On Technology

Never in the history of human society has there been a time like ours when man has attained such a high level of technological achievement. Ironically, never in human history has there been a time like ours when so many people have been so disillusioned, and indeed so bitter about technology. Several thousand years ago Aristotle very soundly observed that before a man can live well, he must be able to live. Technology has made possible a life, and in some ways a better life, for more people than ever before in human history.

Technology has been significant in terms of what it has made possible in the material realm of human existence. Aristotle also observed that all men, by nature, desire to know. I suppose that intellectual curiosity is as deeply rooted a human trait as any that we have, and technology has been humanly significant because of the ways in which it has ministered to this curiosity of ours and because of the intellectual nourishment it has provided us.

Many people in our time have thrilled to our achievements in outer space. The significance of these achievements has never been expressed better than in a recent cartoon drawing in which two friends are sitting under the night sky and looking up at the stars. One says to the other, "You know, many people think that there are other intelligent creatures on planets around every one of those stars." After a pause he continues, "Other people think that we are the only ones . . . . Either way, it's a sobering thought."

Technology has been deeply significant in our time because it has provided us with such sobering thoughts. Yet the bitterness of the disappointment with technology and the resentment toward it are also very understandable. It is hard to believe that with as many advances as we have made in bending nature to human will, we in the United States must still face up to the bitter truth that as many as one-sixth or perhaps even one-fifth of our nation is living in poverty, and that possibly as many as ten or twelve millions of our children go to bed hungry. Our medicine is remarkable, yet the rate of infant mortality in the United States is greater than it is in some ten or fifteen other countries of the world. Our transportation facilities are fantastic; the number of automobiles in the United States is far greater than in any other place in the world, but so also is the number of our traffic fatalities. Our level of production is almost unbelievably high, but so is the rate at which we are polluting our water, our air, and perhaps even the food that we eat. Technology is felt by many, and with good reason, to be deeply dehumanizing.

In our schools we learn that the modern era was ushered in by an industrial revolution several centuries ago. Today many people talk of a *cybernetic revolution* in which computers will free man from the drudgeries of mental labor, just as machinery freed him from the slavery of his body in physical labor. Yet for most human beings, even in this latter part of the twentieth century, the *industrial revolution* has not yet been achieved. For most human beings today, throughout the world and in our country as well, work remains a deadening routine of essentially meaningless operations often directed only to trivial ends. We have devoted a great deal of effort to making work shorter, but comparatively little effort has been expended to make work more meaningful. Perhaps the greatest charge that can be laid at the door of modern technology is that it has made of man only a means to other ends, only a material to be transformed by the technology. Human beings are manipulated as we manipulate things.

Anyone who travels by air today cannot fail to be struck by the dismal contrast between the great technological advance of the jet engine, the airplane itself, and the primitivism involved in the handling of the human passenger, who is made to stand in long lines and shunted from one place to another as though he were a totally inhuman object.

But of course, far and away the most distressing, the most crucial of the issues with which technology confronts us comes from its attainment of unimaginably inhuman levels of destructiveness. Thousands of years ago there lived a Greek philosopher, Heraclitus, of whose works we have left only a few fragments. In one of them he makes a pun on the Greek word *bios,* from which we derive our word 'biology' but which also designates the 'archer's bow'. Heraclitus says of it, "Its name is life, but its work is death." That is what many of us today are saying about science and technology.

The choice between life and death is perhaps as old as human civilization. It is very explicitly formulated in terms that have a startling relevance today in the Book of Deuteronomy when God says to man, "Behold, I have this day set before you the way of life and the way of death; now therefore choose life!" Technology has made the issue of life and death a very real and present issue. Before anything else is said concerning this issue we should remember that the destructive potential with which we are all so desperately concerned is something that has its primary locus within man himself, not within his technology. Whatever has the capacity for good, by that same token has the capacity for evil; the only thing that is absolutely safe is what is absolutely inert and incapable of producing any effect, whether for good or for ill. It is not the bomb that kills people, it is other human beings who kill them. We talk of modern technology as a Frankenstein monster that threatens to destroy us; the symbol is perhaps better than is often appreciated. Frankenstein was not the name of the monster; Frankenstein was the name of the human being who created the monster.

The issues with regard to modern technology might be posed in this way: on the one side, we have a certain exaggerated regard for science and its applications which **Scientism** might be called *scientism*. Scientism is very different indeed from science, very different from the scientific attitude, the scientific mentality, or the scientific method. Scientism is an exaggerated regard, not for what might be attained through the best exercise of the human intellect on human experience, but for what previous applications of intellectual experience have disclosed. Scientism makes of science a fixed creed, and in its very orthodoxy it betrays its fundamentally unscientific character by standing against the continuation of scientific inquiry. Scientism makes the techniques of science the standard of human value. It goes hand-in-hand with a very widespread cult in our time, the *cult of the machine*. Worshippers of the machine seem to think that there is something more humanly significant in the work of human hands than in those hands themselves, as though something made of metal and glass and plastic is somehow intrinsically more scientific or significant than the substance of nerve and blood and bone.

Scientism is a feature of an age which supposes that all fundamental human decisions must be left to experts. It is true that in our time knowledge has become increasingly technical, increasingly difficult of access. But it is also true that there is no way in which a man can live as a man without being a responsible moral agent. This means that he must make his own decisions, consulting expert knowledge where that knowledge is available, but not making the blunder of supposing that he can delegate the responsibility for those decisions to others.

On the opposite side of scientism, and to my mind fully as objectionable, is a kind of hostility to science that might be called *obscurantism*. This reaction to science is marked by a complete alienation from the contents of scientific discovery, from the method of scientific inquiry, and from the whole scientific temper and outlook. The obscurantist supposes that it is somehow more human, more moral, more spiritual to be ignorant and confused. Their numbers abound to the point where our age of fantastic technological achievement is also a time of incredible irrationality, as is shown in the widespread belief in astrology, and in the popularity of magic and various kinds of quackery.

Obscurantism

Quite distinct both from scientism on the one hand, and from obscurantism on the other, is a point of view with regard to technology, which puts it, I think, in its proper place. This is the point of view of *pragmatism,* in which technology is recognized as nothing other than the sum total of all the instrumentalities, all the means that are available to human beings, to attain their ends. *If we are to make reality more ideal, we must give to our ideals more reality.* In other words, our ends must be put into relationship with the means that are required for their attainment. Some time ago one of the greatest of American philosophers, the pragmatist John Dewey, spoke of the organized attack which is made from time to time against science and technology, namely, that they are inherently materialistic and usurp the place properly held by abstract moral precepts. That attack, he says, defines the

Pragmatism

issue we must face. The issue is this: shall we go backwards, or shall we go ahead to discover and put into practice the means by which science and technology can be used for the promotion of human welfare? I believe that this issue is even more crucial in our day than it was in Dewey's, a generation or so ago.

The attacks on technology are, at bottom, attacks on man's capacity to ground his values in the facts of his existence. For a man to turn his back on technology in the name of human values is to make sure that the realization of those values is left to nothing more human than the sheer thrust of prejudice, of power, of tradition, and of whatever special interests might be operative in manipulating both man and his environment to their own special ends.

Great as are the threats to human values from man's ill will as well as from his ignorance and ineptitude, I have sometimes felt that we might be able to cope with the scoundrels if only we are not first destroyed by the fools. It is ironic that there are so many forces at work in the United States in this century which attack technology, which attack the powers of the human mind that create the technology, and which attack the products of the application of the mind, the machines themselves, as though something basic and precious in American life is being threatened by them. After all, there has been a tradition in this country of technology as liberating the human spirit, the tradition of men such as Benjamin Franklin, Thomas Jefferson, Thomas Edison, and many others in our own day. What is fundamental is this: that for all things human, man must be and remain the measure. Our problem does not lie in machines, but in the use that we human beings make of our machines.

There has been much talk in our time of the problems which are posed for us by the population explosion. But there has been another explosion in our time which perhaps is even more fundamentally challenging. That is the explosion of knowledge with its corresponding explosion in the applications, both actual and possible, of that knowledge to human interests. If human values are to be served, we must somehow learn to apply what we have discovered about the world, not only to the means for attaining our ends, but to the ends themselves. We must learn not only to do things in better ways, but also to discern what things are better worth doing.

Whenever there is an attack on technology, an attack on the machine, or on television as a medium, or on the production or assembly line, I believe that we are simply protecting ourselves from the anxieties, and possibly the guilt that would be evoked by our putting the responsibility where it belongs: not on the machine, but on the human beings who design and use the machine. It is up to *us* to determine whether technology is to be used in the service of death or in the service of life.

Some years before we split the atom and probed outward into the reaches of space, that magnificent American poet E. E. Cummings wrote as though he had in mind the coming conquest of space: "all nothing is only our hugest home." The same poem contains the lines:

when skies are hanged and oceans drowned,
the single secret will still be man.

There is no sense in calling for a moratorium on technology, no more sense than there would be in calling for a moratorium on the exercise of the human mind. We have tasted of the fruit of the tree of knowledge once for all. We have left Paradise forever behind us. But if we so choose, we can make use of that knowledge, not to make a heaven on earth, but so to dispose of the resources of the world around us that even the angels can look down and know something of the greatness of man's estate.

On Free Speech

The First Amendment to the Constitution of the United States reads as follows: "Congress shall make no law respecting an establishment of religion, or prohibiting the free exercise thereof, or abridging freedom of speech, or of the press, or the right of the people peaceably to assemble and to petition the government for a redress of grievances." This amendment, the first of the Bill of Rights, has had a long and very honorable history in American life. But recurrently, and today perhaps more than ever before, the rights of free speech, of the free expression of ideas in all media, are coming under attack. This is true not only in totalitarian countries, but also in our own country.

For free speech to have a positive content, it must embrace not only the lack of interference with a man's right to express his ideas but also the availability of opportunities to him for such expression. Today it is possible for a man to reach many millions of others to communicate what he has in his mind. But that possibility remains remote for most of us because of the enormous costs of having *access* to these channels. Access, **Access** therefore, is the first and, in some ways, the most fundamental of the considerations having to do with the preservation of free speech.

More than access is involved. What happens to free speech is similar to what can happen to any of our basic values. First, we lose their meaning; then we begin to lose a sense of their worth; and at last, we lose the value itself. People are not as clear today as they have been at various times in the past about what is meant by free speech, why free speech is important to us, and how free speech can be securely maintained.

To start with, we must recognize that only when we are free to speak our own minds can we emancipate ourselves from

the most insidious and the most destructive of the forms of human bondage, the bondage to fear. It is true that ideas can be dangerous. If anyone were to deny the danger inherent in ideas, I think he would be denying also that ideas have any power for good. But I believe that the danger in ideas challenges us to take a calculated risk. To achieve greatly, a man must dare greatly.

If we try to protect ourselves from the dangers in ideas, we will be losing what is even more precious than our peace of mind. We will be losing any substance and content in our minds. Because truth, in human terms, cannot be defined in terms of a single content. There is no basis for me to say to you that as long as you believe this and that, your beliefs are true, and if you believe such and such, they are false. I can *say* so, but to say so would only be to express *my* beliefs. There is no absolute standard anywhere to which we can appeal. What we can do is to share our ideas and our experiences. *Out of the free interaction of ideas and experiences will emerge something that comes as close to truth as is possible* for the human being.

The nineteenth-century Danish theologian Søren Kierkegaard once remarked that to the basic problems of life there are no answers in the back of the book. Or if there are answers, unfortunately there are a number of different books to choose from. Thus it is that the freedom to express ideas is essential if we are to come as close to truth as our particular situation allows.

Free expression of what is in our minds is important in another way. It is important because unless we have this freedom, no other freedoms are secure. Without the freedom to speak, we cannot call attention to grievances, to needs, to

Engineered Consent

the public interest. In fact, freedom of speech is so fundamental that without it we cannot operate a system of government that is in any recognizable respect democratic. We speak of our political system as being a government by consent. That phrase has meaning only insofar as the consent is freely given. In many parts of the world today and, alas, from time to time and to some degree in the United States as well, consent is not freely given. It is rather an *engineered consent*. There is no doubt that dictators rule with the consent of their subjects. But there is no doubt, either, that such consent is not freely given. It is not the result of a free expression and exchange of information and ideas.

We might make the point in another way by observing that democratic government is self-rule and thus demands a self capable of such rule, a public that is fully informed on public issues. Plato criticized democratic theory with a powerful argument. He pointed out that when it comes to piloting a ship we call for a skilled pilot and not for an ordinary seaman; and if it is a matter of repairing shoes or training horses, we recognize that some people are more able than others. But surely the art of governing a state is more demanding than any of these skills. So, he argues, governments should consist of those who are most able to govern. Plato then goes on to develop his case for aristocracy. We would not be surprised, I am sure, to learn that Plato thought that the people most able to govern were people like himself; namely, philosophers.

To my mind, the weakness in Plato's argument does not lie in the argument itself, but in a hidden assumption it makes: that what we are interested in is making the best decisions, when what we are really interested in is the best *way* of arriving at decisions. As we all know in raising our children, or in relating to students, or in fact, in relationship to ourselves and those around us, a man cannot mature, cannot fulfill his potentialities, cannot become all he is capable of becoming, unless he is given the opportunity to *make his own decisions,* even though, conceivably, other people might be able to make better decisions for him. A man cannot make his own decisions if he has no basis on which to decide, and if he is denied access to the channels by which he can express his ideas to others.

The principles of free speech are often obscured, particularly the fundamental consideration that the right to speak one's mind freely becomes especially important when the opinions which one holds are unpopular ones. Everyone welcomes the expression of popular opinion; I suppose that is what it means to say that they are popular. But there is no such thing as a right to free speech unless it extends precisely to the ideas that are not widely shared.

To be sure, there are limits to this freedom, as to all freedoms. One limit, formulated in the last century by John Stuart Mill in a classic essay, *On Liberty,* is this: a man's freedom must stop short of actions which will interfere with the freedom of other people. The great Justice Oliver Wendell Holmes said that the right of free expression is limited when there is a clear and present danger in that expression. A man may not shout "fire" in a crowded place, a man may not make jokes about bombs on an airplane. In neither case can he appeal to the right to free speech; it is clear that speaking under those conditions will affect other values, other rights, and other liberties.

There is a confusion in our time as to the conditions under which free speech may be exercised. The right to express yourself means that there must be some time and place when you can give voice to what is in your mind. It does *not* mean that you can choose whatever time and place you like. It does not mean that you can come into my home, or into my classroom, or into my meeting place to express your ideas. It means that you have a right as much as I to a forum, but not that you have a right to *my* forum.

I remember when a number of us who were very much concerned about the crisis in the Middle East and the fate of the state of Israel organized a meeting. A member of the Arab Students' League demanded the right to speak on that occasion. Many people supposed that the principles of free speech guaranteed him that right. But they were mistaken. To be sure, the principles of free speech guarantee him the right to have *his* meeting at some time and place of his choosing, and to express himself freely then and there, whatever the content of his ideas. But they do not give him license to interfere with the rights of others.

Symbolic Speech

The form in which this problem presents itself to us most commonly, most distressingly, is in connection with what might be called *symbolic speech*. This is the kind of speech which consists not so much of words as of gestures, and maybe even actions and other symbols of various kinds. The principles of free speech must surely protect symbolic speech as they protect any other form, provided that such symbolic speech is nonviolent, is civil in its forms—that is, provided that it takes place within a shared framework of legality by which alone free speech and our other freedoms can be secured. From the very beginning democratic political theory has rested on a moral basis. This has been fundamental to the democratic political philosophy of John Locke, of Thomas

Jefferson, and of many theorists since. They held that the law of the state does not define the highest form of law; man has a conscience and he may have religious convictions. In other words, he has other basic values with reference to which he enjoys the right and even the moral obligation to judge the actions of his government. Yet there is a fundamental paradox in this moral basis of democracy. The *paradox of political morality* might be expressed in this way: if each man enjoys the right of a personal veto over any law which does not accord with his moral perception, there can be no such thing as a rule of law.

One generalization which can be made from the history of tyranny is that freedoms are abridged and ultimately destroyed, not in the name of tyranny, but in the name of some principle which usually presents itself as a moral principle. Symbolic speech, therefore, like other forms of speech, is limited by all those conditions through which it may interfere with the rights of others. It is one thing for a man to express a dissenting opinion; it is another thing for him to express that dissent in such a way as to coerce not only the opinions, but also the actions of others.

There is a very human tendency in all of us to look for *moral bargains,* to enjoy the gratification, the self-esteem of adhering to our principles, without having to pay the price that principles sometimes demand, whether that price is unpopularity, or opposition, or perhaps the hostility of those around us. The right to speak my mind implies that I have a right to be heard. But it does not imply that I have a right to your agreement. You may hear, and disagree so strongly as to have contempt for me. If I choose to abide by my principles, I shall have to face up to that contempt as well.

There is a magnificent passage in the *Analects* of Confucius, written millennia ago: "The wise man," Confucius says, "engages in politics, not because he expects his principles to prevail, but because it is in accord with his principles to engage in politics."

No matter how clear the meaning of free speech may be, and no matter how intensely we prize it, the price of this liberty, as of all our liberties, is eternal vigilance; vigilance in keeping open the channels for expression and in maximizing access to those channels; and vigilance for the adherence to the principles of due process, since the means that we choose quite often betray the ends which those means are intended to serve. We *will never secure a moral outcome either for ourselves or for our society by turning to immoral means; we will never truly serve humane ends by inhuman means.* We must be particularly vigilant, it seems to me, when the right to express an opinion is only slightly infringed, when it happens to only a few people, particularly people we might not care very much about, and when it is infringed with regard to ideas that we are hostile to. If I may apply the words of the Gospel to this context, "as ye did it unto one of these the least of my brothers, ye have done it unto me." *No man's freedoms are secure if any man's freedoms are denied.*

Shortly before the French Revolution, the great French philosopher Jean Jacques Rousseau wrote an enormously influential book, *The Social Contract.* The opening sentence in that book is that men are born free, yet they are everywhere in chains. I don't believe that we are born free; freedom is an attainment. We are born with the capacity and the desire for freedom. As John Dewey has said in our time, each generation must achieve that freedom for itself. There is another philosopher, who died only a few years ago, Martin Buber of the Hebrew University in Jerusalem, who emphasized how essential it is that each of us, as the individual human beings that we are, commit ourselves to our values and our principles. "Without you and me," he said, "the most glorious institution is a lie." Free speech is a glorious institution indeed. It is for us to make it a truth.

On Unreason

No doubt many of us have often felt that the whole world has gone mad. It probably has seemed to us that events in very recent times are repeated expressions of this madness. We are not the first generation which has felt that our fellow men have taken leave of their senses. About a hundred years ago the Norwegian playwright Henrik Ibsen presented in his *Peer Gynt* a scene in a madhouse to which Peer Gynt comes in his travels. The director of the madhouse tells him, "There has been a revolution in the world: all persons who, up until 11:00 last night, were known as mad have now become normal in conformity with reason in its newest phase. And if you consider the matter farther, it is clear that from that very hour our so-called wise men all went mad. Reason is dead."

In the time that separates us from Ibsen's *Peer Gynt* there have been a number of forces at work to attack reason, if not to destroy it. These attacks have sometimes come from religion, from those who thought, as Immanuel Kant put it several centuries ago, that reason must be limited in order to make room for faith. The attackers failed to recognize that faith is not a matter of feeblemindedness or irrationality. Reason has been attacked also from the side of politics, from those who, in their bitter awareness of the injustices our society has perpetrated on the culturally deprived, have imagined that if we abandon reason, the works of reason, and the life of the mind, because these things are seen as the privileges of an elite, then we have done something on behalf of the minorities. In this connection, for instance, there has been an extraordinary degradation of the English language in our time. I do not mean that our writers cannot use the language as in former days, or even that our young men and women are not as aware as ever they were of the subtleties of the language.

But people somehow suppose that it is morally wrong, or at least politically improper, for them to use language to the full, as though by doing so they would identify themselves not with the victims of injustice, but with the elite that is guilty of the injustice.

The attack on reason in our time has come from another source too. It has come from the intellectuals themselves. It has come from faculties and from students. It has come not only from the enemies of the life of the mind, but even from those who one would suppose are themselves dedicated to the life of the mind. In the universities it is to be found in the demand for what is called relevance, but a relevance which is often so narrowly circumscribed and so dogmatically fixed beforehand, that it seems to many to be contrary to the claims of reason.

Ours is a society in which what ought to be, what can be, what has been at various times in human history the instrument of reason, has become instead a device for *magic*. Words, symbols, signs, and actions which could be the carriers of various kinds of intellectual contents, have all too often been reduced in our time to slogans, gestures, posters, signs, and demonstrations, as though somehow, if we stand before the closed door and call out "Open, Sesame!," the magic formula itself will open the door.

All these attacks on reason have given rise to a number of substitutes for reason, or at least to patterns which claim to replace reason. Of these, probably the most well known, the most significant, and certainly in many ways the most **Activism** dangerous is the *call to action*. There is also a kind of magic involved in this call to action. When you stand before the door and cry out "Open, Sesame!" and the door does not open, it is very human to kick the door in frustration and anger. Action thus becomes another kind of magic, because in this perspective of unreason, it attempts to achieve goals not directly and reasonably, but in magical and mysterious ways.

In political life, the most monstrous example is *terror*. **Terror** Among the many possible characterizations of the twentieth century, and it is, I think, one of the great tragedies and one of the most challenging problems of our time, is that ours is the century of terror. It is a century, that is to say, in which men take action not in the form of struggling to overcome their problems but in the form of taking up arms instead against some bystander, some innocent person or group that is not even a party to the problems. The magical belief is that if only we act somewhere, on someone, in a sufficiently determined fashion, something will have to give. You drop your coin into the machine, and when you don't get your drink or whatever it is you had bargained for, you kick the machine in the infantile and unreasonable belief that the kick will get you what you want.

Maybe the most general description which can be given of this species of unreason, the call to action regardless of *what* action, is this: we imagine that if only our means are sufficiently extreme, then the ends served by those means must be correspondingly radical. This notion, I believe, is responsible for the great human cost of this kind of unreason. Quite often very extreme means, in which many human lives may be lost, accomplish at best only the most trivial ends. They do so because we are wrapped up in the fantasies of unreason, fantasies which somehow persuade us that we can get everything that we want all at once, if only we recite the appropriate "Open, Sesame!" The American philosopher John Dewey put the matter very simply: "The best is the worst enemy of the better."

Feeling

There is a second kind of unreason in our time, very different from the unreason of the activist; that is the unreason which consists in putting forth the claims of *feeling*. It should be said at the outset that all of us owe a debt of gratitude to the hippies, and to similar people and movements in our time. For in putting forward the claims of feeling, they have liberated us in many ways from a certain drabness, a certain grayness of our experience. There is a color in our lives today, a richness and excitement of pattern, of form, of texture, which I think we have not known for many decades. I think it is not unreasonable to expect that in the years and decades to come we will be able to look back on this time as one of a great freeing of creative energies and artistic sensibilities.

Yet feeling has a way of growing on what it feeds on. It has a way of moving beyond sensitivity, beyond the exploration of the values which direct experience affords, into a kind of frenzy—the *psychedelic frenzy* not just of the drug cults but of many aspects of our lives—a frenzy which does not open our sensibilities to the flow of experience but deadens our sensitivity, so that we drown in our feelings.

A long time ago Plato analyzed the human psyche in terms of the myth or metaphor of a chariot drawn by the fiery steeds of passion with reason as the charioteer holding the steeds in check. This conception of a fundamental duality between passion on the one side and reason on the other has been enormously influential in the history of our civilization. That influence, it seems to me, has not always been for the good. Without passion life has no savor, and most of us would feel it is not worth living. If we begin by contrasting reason with the passions, it is not to be wondered at that reason comes out second best.

There is another way in which the psyche can be analyzed. One of the exponents of this other way of conceptualizing man's nature is Sigmund Freud, the father of psychoanalysis. For Freud, the proper contrast is not between reason on the one hand and emotion on the other, but between *rational emotion* and *irrational emotion*. Reason cannot deny the claims of feeling. It would be unreasonable to do so. What reason must demand is that our feelings have a rational basis and that they relate to the real world. It is rational to feel fear in the presence of a cobra, but it is not rational to be afraid of a harmless grass snake.

There is another kind of unreason in our time which, in part, takes advantage of the call to action, and in part shares also the claims of feeling. This is the retreat to *subjectivity*. According to this approach, what is really significant in my life has its locus inside me, away from other human beings, and most especially, away from a society which I experience only as inhibiting me, as controlling me, as imposing all sorts of restrictions on me, as transforming my simple nature into something artificial, something which negates all that makes my life meaningful.

Here also is a delusion which Ibsen has called to our attention very dramatically in his *Peer Gynt*. When Peer Gynt comes to the madhouse, he feels that while *he* is himself, the madmen around him are, as we would say, beside themselves. But he is told that it is exactly the contrary. It is here in the madhouse that men are most themselves, "themselves and nothing but themselves, sailing with outspread sails of self,

Subjectivism

each man shuts himself up in a barrel of self, the barrel stopped up with a bung of self, and seasoned in a well of self; no one has a tear for anyone else's troubles, no one cares what anyone else thinks. We are our selves, in thought and voice, our selves up to the very limit." That is madness—to be yourself, to be lost only in your own subjectivity, to know nothing and to care nothing of what is happening to other people, and of what is happening in the world around you.

The Persecution and Assassination of Jean-Paul Marat as Performed by the Inmates of the Asylum of Charenton Under the Direction of the Marquis de Sade, a play by Peter Weis, has a scene in which the Marquis in the madhouse tells us about our subjectivity: "You swim," he says, "all huddled up alone with your ideals about the world, which no longer fit the world outside, and why should you care about the world outside?—for me, the only reality is imagination, the world inside myself."

That, I think, is the great unreason of our time, and perhaps of all times. It is what Bertrand Russell once called "subjectivist madness." It is *the madness of supposing that I define reality.* It is the madness of supposing that the fantasy world of my own making is more real than God's world of people and things around me. It is in fact the madness of mistaking myself for a god, and of mistaking my feelings of this particular moment for the whole compass of all of reality.

One of the forms of unreason in our time is to turn our backs on history. The American philosopher George Santayana once observed that the penalty for ignoring history is that we are condemned to repeat it. Subjectivism denies history. It does so, not because in its critical attitudes and skepticism it finds a credibility gap between its own beliefs and what the historian presents, but because it imagines that the whole of history is irrelevant to the present moment. Subjectivism also imagines that the future consequences of our present choices are irrelevant to this present.

These are the forms of unreason—the unreason of a call to action without knowing what to do or why, the unreason of the claims of feeling without knowing what we are to feel or why, the unreason of subjectivity without an awareness of how each person relates to other human beings and to the world around him. To escape all these unreasons we must restore to ourselves and in our social practice a sense of *the intellectual virtues—respect for opinions that differ from our own, respect for empirical evidence, and respect for rational argument.*

There is an axiom which has been stated by philosophers from the time of Socrates onward, and reinforced by such students of men's madness as contemporary psychiatrists. It is, I believe, *the* philosophical axiom: that to understand is not necessarily to forgive, but something even better: *to understand is to transcend,* to go beyond. To grasp the truth is to free ourselves from the bondage to which our ignorance of the truth, our unreason, subjects us—to free ourselves from the alternatives to reason: violence, frenzy, and, in the last resort, madness.

In the religious symbolism of our western tradition man is represented as having been created in the image of God, then falling from grace and innocence because he disobeyed God's law and tasted of the fruit of the tree of knowledge. The great medieval philosopher Moses Maimonides put forth the doctrine to which I wholeheartedly subscribe, that man's reason is not a consequence of his Fall, that on the contrary, it is precisely because of our reason that we are in the image of

God. When we live a life of unreason, even the angels weep for us. If we make use of the gifts of the intellect with which we have been endowed, it may still be that our reason will not suffice for us to solve the many problems with which we are confronted. But whether we fail or succeed, whether we live or die, if we live by the powers of the mind, we can take a reasoned pride in the dignity of being human.

On Loneliness

There is no one who does not know what loneliness is. Yet it seems that the more significant an experience is for us, the more difficult we find it is to put the experience into words. What is loneliness? How do we come to be lonely? What is happening in our lives that makes so many of us lonely?

To start with, we can say quite confidently that to be lonely is by no means the same thing as to be alone. There are many different ways of being alone; one of them is something we call *privacy*. We all feel that there is an area in our lives in which only *we* have a part to play. Someone else can enter only if we invite them to come be with us. If we are unhappy because of loneliness, it most certainly is *not* because we are enjoying too much privacy. Justice Louis Brandeis once said of privacy that it is the most cherished, the most prized value among civilized beings. Yet privacy is becoming more and more difficult for any of us to secure. Loneliness is something very different from the privacy we all seek. **Privacy**

There is another way of being alone. We sometimes seek not only privacy but also *seclusion*. A person has a work of creation to perform, and we can create only when we are alone. Sometimes the work of creation is painful (Nietzsche said about it that the pain makes both hens and poets cackle). So we seclude ourselves in order to bring forth something that we have within ourselves. That is not being lonely, it is only being alone when we want to be. **Seclusion**

There is still another way of being alone. When someone is discharging a responsibility that he cannot delegate to anyone else, he feels the burden of *constructive loneliness*. Charlie Brown once said that the loneliest place on earth is the pitcher's mound. Although we may feel that it is a childish responsibility after all which Charlie bears on his shoulders, I **Constructive Loneliness**

think there is none of us who does not know the burden of this constructive loneliness as we discharge a responsibility which no one can discharge in our place. I have in mind the image of Abraham Lincoln, sitting, the familiar bowed figure wrapped in his shawl, knowing that on his shoulders rest the burdens of the maintenance of the Union, and feeling lonely in that responsibility. This is a special kind of loneliness, and it is essential to maturity.

In the loneliness from which we all suffer there is another element which is not present in any of these ways of being alone. It is the element of *withdrawal*. We are lonely when we experience ourselves as having lost something precious, which has been withdrawn. In all loneliness there is a good deal of the feeling conveyed in the words of the popular folk song of our time "Where Have All the Flowers Gone?" For my generation, that feeling was conveyed in a poem by A. E. Housman in *A Shropshire Lad:*

Withdrawal

> With rue my heart is laden
>   For golden friends I had,
> For many a rose-lipt maiden
>   And many a lightfoot lad.
>
> By brooks too broad for leaping
>   The lightfoot boys are laid;
> The rose-lipt girls are sleeping
>   In fields where roses fade.

I am lonely when I feel that those who were once close to me, those whom I loved and who loved me, are no longer a part of my world.

There is an even more poignant poem of loneliness, "The Love Song of J. Alfred Prufrock," written some decades ago by one of the great poets of the English language in the twentieth century, T. S. Eliot. Prufrock is a lonely man, and a man who knows the loneliness of others. In the poem he wonders whether he can describe significant experiences in his life:

Shall I say, I have gone at dusk through narrow streets
And watched the smoke that rises from the pipes
Of lonely men in shirt-sleeves, leaning out of windows?. . .

This passage summons up the image of a man who feels that life has passed him by, a man who has withdrawn from life. There is sound and movement on the street below and he cannot quite bring himself to leave it altogether. Yet there is no more for him to do than to watch from above while he is wrapping himself in the smoke from his pipe, perhaps to cover himself with a haze of fantasy, as early in the poem a yellow fog wrapped round the house, and as at the end of the poem he says

We have lingered in the chambers of the sea
By sea-girls wreathed with seaweed red and brown
Till human voices wake us, and we drown.

There is a story of a parent talking to a teenager. "You know what the trouble is with you teenagers today, you're all so full of apathy. You know what that means?" The teen replies, "No, and I couldn't care less." The fact is, of course, that our young today know very well, and they care very deeply. Yet there is a loneliness which results from the withdrawal that seems to be the pattern in our society. We remove ourselves from one another.

This is symbolized by the changing styles of the dance in the United States. There was a time when dance was a group activity, as in the square dance, the Virginia Reel, and the round dances of the various folk idioms which make up the core of

American culture. At about the time of World War I these group dances were replaced by couple dances; that was the great age of the fox-trot and the waltz. But at about the time of World War II, the couple dance was, in its turn, replaced by a dance in which each individual does his own thing, in which there is no contact, in which even eye contact is presumably no longer important. There must be some reason why the young still dance these dances, and I am sure the reason is not so very different from the one that impelled us to dance in our styles. Yet there is a distance and, it seems to me, a sense of loneliness that play a very marked part in the dance today.

Why should we withdraw from other people when we all want so desperately to be with other people? The answer is very largely conveyed in one word: we are *afraid*. We are **Fear** afraid of being rejected. How do I dare to offer my friendship to you, if you will tell me that you do not want it? That would be so cruel and crushing a blow that I protect myself by telling you, in effect, "You can't fire me, I quit!" The irony is that in human relations we often quit before even beginning the job, and then, for such is the deviousness of the human mind, we somehow persuade ourselves that in this way we have really arrived at job security.

There are other fears that operate in us. I may be afraid, not just of being rejected, but also of being accepted, because I may be found to be inadequate. Or, I may be afraid, not that you will reject me nor that you will find me inadequate, but that you will find me very adequate, and then I may find myself committed to you when all I had in mind was just a pleasant evening. Suddenly I am invited to your home, I meet your family, I am involved in this and that; so I protect myself from the commitment which I do not dare to undertake by withdrawing. Even if I dare enter upon the commitment, I may be afraid that I will be exhausted. I just haven't enough strength, I'm going to be squeezed dry. Or I may be afraid that I am going to be in subjection, and will no longer be able to call my soul my own. If I have a roommate, I can't turn on the light when I want, and I can't turn off the light when I want, I can't sleep when I want, I can't wake when I want, I can't listen to music—I can't do anything when I want. So I'm not going to have a roommate; but I'm so lonely!

Dehumanization

In addition to these fears which keep me apart from others, there are many patterns in operation in our society which would keep us apart even if we were willing to be together. Society is in many ways *dehumanizing*. We relate to one another, not in terms of our *identities,* not in terms of what makes me the person that I am and you the particular human being that you are, but we relate to one another in terms of our *identifications,* in terms of marks which are quite superficial and perhaps altogether arbitrary, marks by which I can be distinguished from other people and by which you can put me in my place; I have a pocketful of identifications. When you relate to me in terms of those identifications and not in terms of the person that I am, then I feel lonely, because I have not known another human being and no other human being has known me.

In our society we go even further. We *exploit* one another in ways that dehumanize us. I remember seeing an ad in an airport, in words that attracted my human interests and concerns. It read: "In a world in which everyone is looking out for himself, isn't it nice to know that someone cares about you?" At the bottom was "Acme Automobile Rentals." It would indeed be nice to know that someone cares about me, but the sponsorship was the giveaway: no one really cared about me. I was dehumanized. I was only a customer, someone who could pay for a service. Even if the service were all I could expect to buy, I would still feel lonely, because no one related to me as a human being.

Many people feel that we are dehumanized because our society is so highly technological, and because in a fundamental way machines can relate only to other machines, while human beings can relate only to other human beings. In my own field of education, for example, in recent years we have begun to explore the possibilities of teaching machines. I feel that those possibilities hold out very great promise; I am a warm advocate of the use of technology in all the ways that our imaginations and intellects will disclose to us for the purposes of instruction. But I believe also that *instruction* is one thing and *education* is another. There is a process of the transmission and processing of data and information in which machines should be used in place of human beings. Everything that can be done by machines ought to be done by machines so as to leave human beings free for their distinctively human potentials. But there is a process of education, of growth, in which a human being can share only when he shares it with another human being. I have sometimes wished that we would develop not only teaching machines, but also learning machines, and then hook them up to each other in a closed circuit, so that somewhere, in another place, a few human beings could sit and talk to one another, educate one another, and, above all, counter their basic human loneliness.

We always reach out for other human beings. I believe that one of the tragedies of our time is that if we have no other way of relating to others, we do so by violence. We somehow manage to feel that we have expressed our humanity and are relating to others in their humanity, even if we are engaged in destroying one another. Linus in talking to Charlie Brown about a little girl who has moved in down the street says, "I was watching her move in, and she came up to me and asked me if I wanted to be friends, and I didn't know what to say—so I slugged her." That is a childish response; we can understand that a more mature response would have put too great a demand on his young personality. It is not so easy to be a friend. Yet if we choose the easier way, if we suppose that we can relate with the other only through violence, we pay the price of feeling lonely.

I have been describing ways in which the conditions of our society make people lonely, but I believe that there are other and more fundamental dimensions of loneliness which cut across the differences between one society and another. I believe that there is a dimension of loneliness which is a universal component of the human experience. To understand this necessary loneliness, we must distinguish between what might be called *contingent* loneliness and *existential* loneliness. Contingent loneliness is temporary and correctable. It is the kind of loneliness that we experience under special circumstances, and it can be expected to disappear when circumstances change. A child is sick, he hears his friends playing in the street below, and he feels lonely. But the illness runs its course; he rises up from the sickbed and joins his friends. A man travels, he is away from his home and his loved ones, and he feels lonely. But his travels end, he returns home, and his loneliness is over.

We find it hard sometimes to accommodate even contingent loneliness; though it is only temporary, we find it dif-

Contingent Loneliness

ficult to tolerate the unhappiness even for a short period of time. Motels and hotels sometimes advertise that they provide a home away from home. But why should I have a home away from home? My wife would not like it. And she is entirely in the right. When a man is away from those he loves and who love him, he will experience loneliness. But it is a contingent loneliness, and when time passes and circumstances change, it will yield to the joy of reunion.

Existential Loneliness

There is another kind of loneliness, *existential loneliness,* which belongs to the condition of man as a human being. Friends inevitably drift apart; if they do not, it must be that they are holding one another so close that it is no longer an expression of friendship. Children grow up, and they can never go home again. Much of the loneliness that is experienced by students, by children of all ages, is an inescapable part, an existential component of the process of maturing, growing up, and building a life for themselves. In the same way there is the existential loneliness not only for the children but also for their parents. As the children leave, the parents know and must come to terms with a loneliness that is a part of being human. This kind of loneliness has no antidote. We cannot solve this kind of problem; we can only cope with it, just as we cannot solve the other fundamental human problems of aging or of facing up to death. But we can learn to cope with these problems.

There are people who believe that the loneliness of our time is a consequence of our loss of faith. They tell us that when man knew himself to be the center of the universe he never felt lonely. There is a beautiful passage in the book of Psalms in which the Psalmist writes: "Whither shall I go from Your spirit, where shall I fly from Your presence? If I ascend to heaven,

You are there, and if I make my bed in hell, You are there. If I take the wings of the morning and dwell in the outermost parts of the sea, even there Your hands shall lead me, Your right hand shall hold me." People say that if only we could retain that faith, there would be no occasion for us to feel lonely. Yet it seems to me that there never was any such thing as "that old-time religion." The very same Psalmist who wrote these beautiful lines about God always being present with him, is the one who wrote the words spoken by Jesus on the cross, "My God, my God, why have You forsaken me?" There has always been this struggle of faith; man has always needed to wrestle with his angel. Man has always had the task of coping with loneliness, with the feeling that what he has known and loved in this world is no longer with him.

I believe that the task of coping with loneliness is always with us because the most fundamental alienation which a man experiences is the alienation from himself. Scripture enjoins "Love your neighbor as yourself." But how can I love my neighbor if I do not love myself? How can anyone understand me if I do not understand myself? How can anyone accept me if I do not accept myself, how can anyone enjoy being with me if I cannot enjoy being with myself?

In one of his plays Oscar Wilde has a character remark that to learn to love oneself is to lay the foundations for a lifelong romance. It may be that the man who has learned to be only his own friend has not risen to the full stature of his humanity. At any rate, he will not suffer that diminution of spirit which we all know as loneliness.

On Mental Health

Mental illness remains one of the very great problems of our time. *As many hospital beds are occupied by the victims of mental illness as are occupied by patients suffering from all other diseases put together.* This statistic includes only those illnesses that are so severe as to call for hospitalization. There is none of us who does not know in some measure what it is to suffer from mental illness. For such illness consists essentially in our finding it impossible to face up to reality, whether it be the reality outside us or the real world within. About a century ago Dostoevskii, in his *Notes from the Underground,* characterized our relationship to that inner and outer reality in terms which are as true today as they were when he wrote them. "We are all divorced from life," he wrote, "we are all cripples, every one of us, more or less; we are so divorced from it that we feel at once a sort of loathing for real life and so cannot bear to be reminded of it. Why, we are almost come to looking upon real life as an effort, almost as hard work, and we are all privately agreed that it is better in books." Today we might say in movies or on television.

One of the most important aspects of mental health consists of our capacity to express our *feelings.* Unfortunately, many people regard feelings as being somehow unmanly, or unworthy of us, or even as immoral and altogether to be condemned. In the Book of Matthew, for instance, we find, "You have heard that it was said to the men of old, 'You shall not commit adultery'; but I say to you that every one who looks at a woman lustfully has already committed adultery with her in his heart." There are people who condemn feeling as though having the feeling is equivalent to performing the action, and as though every shade of feeling, however slight and tenuous, is equivalent to the most extreme form of the feeling. As long

Feelings

75

as we conceive of our feelings in this way, as long as we suppose that the feeling is the same as the action, and that every shade of feeling is the same as its most extreme forms, it is no wonder that we do not allow ourselves to experience or express our feelings.

Long ago Plato discussed diseases of the mind and held that basically they result from a lack of control over our feelings, as is characteristic of madness and ignorance: "In whatever state a man experiences either of them [excessive pain or pleasure], that state may be called disease, and excessive pains and pleasures [the whole spectrum of our feelings, we would say] are justly to be regarded as the greatest diseases to which the soul is liable. For a man who is in great joy, or in great pain, in his unseasonable eagerness to attain the one and to avoid the other is not able to see or hear anything rightly, but he is mad, and is at the time utterly incapable of any participation in reason."

There is something in what Plato says here, of course, but I think also that he is profoundly mistaken, and mistaken in a very dangerous way, in giving us the impression that if we so much as express what we feel, we have taken leave of our senses. The truth is very nearly the opposite. Mental illness is very much more a matter of *not* acknowledging our feelings and expressing them. Of course, it is one thing to *express* feeling, to put it into words and gestures, to bring it out where we can see it and know it for what it is, and it is quite another thing to *act* on our feelings. Mental health does not demand that whenever we feel like committing adultery, it is healthy to go ahead and do it, and whenever we feel like killing someone, it is healthy for us to go ahead and do that. What is crucial to mental health is for us to recognize our feelings as facts about ourselves; mental health is less a matter of the capacity to *control* ourselves than it is the capacity to arrive at an *integration,* an inner unity in which lack of control is no longer a danger.

Anger

What Matthew declares about feelings of love, he declares also about feelings of *anger:* "You have heard that it was said to the men of old 'You shall not kill, and whoever kills shall be liable to judgment'; but I say to you that every one who is angry with his brother shall be liable to judgment, whoever insults his brother shall be liable, and whoever says 'You fool' shall be liable to the fires of hell." The fact is that there are a great many fools in the world; it is a matter of mental health to recognize that sometimes we are moved to anger by folly. It is important to our health to express that anger. We do not need to *act out* the anger, only to acknowledge it, to recognize the part which it is playing in ourselves, so that we can assess its relationship to both the external and the internal reality.

Aggression

There are, as a matter of fact, two very different psychological processes which find expression in feelings of anger. One of them is essential to life itself; we might call it *aggression.* This is the capacity to pursue goals in the face of obstacles, whatever those obstacles might be, with a certain kind of resoluteness and determination. It is a capacity to bring our energies to bear on behalf of our goals, in spite of obstacles that prevent our moving toward them. Aggression is very different from another complex of psychic states and processes, which we might call *hostility.* Unlike aggression, hostility is not constructive, not a movement toward a goal; it is purely destructive, and it destroys itself as well as its target. It is usually displaced from its proper object: we kick the cat when we get home or we are furious with our wife and

Hostility

children, even though in the course of our activities during the day it was not they who stood in our way. Moreover our hostility is likely to be disproportionate to what is called for in order to move the obstacle aside. Above all, it is likely to be uncontrolled—the hostility takes hold of me to the point where it is not serving my ends. On the contrary, I myself become an instrument to a destructive anger which has become an end in itself.

In Scripture we are told to hate the sin but not the sinner. That is what it means, I think, to be aggressive when aggression is called for by our values and principles and ideals, but at the same time not to allow ourselves to be consumed by hostility.

There is another important component of mental health, and that is *authenticity*—the quality of being honest with and true to ourselves. So much of our lives is occupied in acting roles which have been assigned to us by others, roles which are called for by the situations in which we find ourselves, and roles which we impose on ourselves. The more of our psychic energies that go into the performance of these roles, the more we feel that there is something unreal and artificial in our lives; the more, that is to say, we feel that we are living, not our own lives, but the lives of other people. This is what is so destructive about conformity: not that there is any intrinsic virtue in being different, but there most decidedly is virtue, or at least health, in being genuinely the human beings that we are. Thoreau tells us that if a man is out of step with his fellows, it may be that he hears a different drummer. Let him march to the music that he hears. I think it is essential to a person's mental health that he march to the music that he hears. Otherwise he can never keep in step with himself.

But I think it should also be recognized that there is a limit

Authenticity

to what we think of as honesty. There is a limit to how much we can expose of ourselves, and how much we can let authenticity guide our conduct and express our attitudes. It quite often happens these days that people relate to us in very inhuman ways, then imagine that they are offering a justification for this inhumanity by telling us, "Well, that's the way I really felt." The fact that someone is being honest in his hatred does not make the hatred any the less destructive either to him or to his victims. Sometimes I think I would rather that people be not quite so honest with me, or at any rate, I would rather that they would not use a claim to honesty as a justification or rationalization for the cruelties they practice upon me.

It is well to remember that to be truly authentic, a man must be true, not only to what he is, but also to all that he is becoming, to all that he might become. There is a charming story written some decades ago by Max Beerbohm called *The Happy Hypocrite*, which has a profoundly important moral. A man who had led a rather dissolute life went to the theater and fell in love with a beautiful young actress whom he saw on the stage. He went backstage after the performance and proposed marriage to her, but she took one look at him and said, "No. You have the face of a dissolute man; I could only marry a man with the face of an angel." Accordingly, he went to a maker of masks and said, "Fashion me a mask of an angel and contrive so that it shall fit perfectly over my own face." So it was done. He put on the mask and went back to the theater. When she saw him with the face of an angel, she fell in love with him immediately, and they went off and lived very happily together for some time. But a discarded mistress tracked him down and demanded that he return with her. He said, "No, I have been happy here with my bride and here I shall remain." She said, "If you do not come with me, I will expose you before her," and he replied, "Do what you must." So she called out the wife and said, "See what manner of man you have married!" and tore off his mask. Behold, his face had grown to resemble it. Although Beerbohm does not spell out the moral, I think we might say in this context that for the sake of our mental health and the happiness of those around us, it might be well if we were to learn to lie a little bit—especially because the lie for love may become the truth. There is a remark of one of the rabbis that the punishment which a man must suffer for pretending to be a saint is that eventually he really gets to be one.

Mental health depends upon something more: not only upon our capacity to express our feelings, both of affection and aggression, without necessarily acting them out, and our capacity to be authentic; but mental health also depends upon maintaining a certain system of *defenses*. Many people today seem to regard being defensive as engaging in some kind of unhealthy, improper behavior. But people need defenses; without them we are defenseless. What is important is that our defenses be flexible and varied, and that they relate realistically to the actual situations in which we find ourselves. Too often, because we feel ourselves to be vulnerable we deny ourselves the human warmth which we so desperately want. We do so because of our fears of being rejected, of being found wanting, or of being put into subjection to the will of another, so that we can no longer call our soul our own. All our defenses then set to work to protect us against the dangers that seem to be confronting us. Unfortunately, they are defenses that not only protect us from the imagined enemy, but also alienate us from our friends, and ultimately from

Defenses

ourselves. It is as though I am so afraid of losing my privacy that I will not let anyone through the door of my house. Like a medieval knight I stand guard at the moat and gate of my castle and pour hot oil down on the head of anyone so rash as to come seeking admission. Such a posture means that I have condemned myself to loneliness. It means also that I have brought myself very close to the borders of mental illness.

Perhaps we could say about psychological defenses what might also be said about systems of national defense: so often the trouble is that national defenses are ways to fight the last war, not to protect us from the real dangers of the present or emerging future. So often, they make demands for an impossible share of our national budget. Sometimes, even, they are no longer under civilian control. Mental health calls for defenses, but it calls for rational and realistic defenses in the service of our psyche, and not those which, in fact, act against our own interests.

Acceptance

If I had to put into a single word what mental health consists in, what it depends upon, I think the one that I would choose is the word *acceptance*. Acceptance is the capacity to accept human beings for what they are instead of judging them, and exhorting them to change and become other human beings. It makes us able to say, "This is what you are, and whatever you are, you are the most significant part of my world, as I hope I can be of yours." Mental health means especially the capacity to accept *ourselves* as we are and as we want to become. To be truly healthy I must resist the temptation to weigh my worth all the time. This does not mean abandoning my ideals—quite the contrary, it means recognizing that failure as well as success is a part of man's nature, and that it is the nature of ideals that actualities will always fall short of them. It means recognizing that we are human beings, not gods. When man deceives himself into supposing that he is a god, he invariably behaves like a beast, or he sinks into the depths of mental illness.

We have attained to mental health in the degree to which we are capable of laughing at ourselves, not in hostility, but in compassion, in seeing our shortcomings, in seeing our immaturities, in seeing even our childishness. There is a beautiful line in the prologue to Goethe's *Faust:* " 'Tis not that we leave childhood as we age, but that we learn at last what children we remain." It is a part of health to recognize the child within, and to accept that childlike quality as the source of creativity, imagination, spontaneity, and joy. To be healthy is to see ourselves in perspective: to know our shortcomings, but to know also our greatness.

On this point, as on so many others, I know of no place where the essential has been so eloquently put as in Scripture. The Book of Psalms asks, "What is man, that you are mindful of him?—the son of man, that you visit him?" And it is able to continue in the same breath, "Yet you have made him but a little lower than the angels and have crowned him with honor and with glory." It is this capacity to see that man is nothing but a man after all, and to experience also the greatness of being human, which constitutes mental health.

On Aging

The great burden of aging is loneliness. The loneliness of the young always has its limits. The young know that sooner or later loneliness will be over: "Journeys end in lovers' meeting, every wise man's son doth know." But for the aging, journeys have another end. It is intrinsic to the universal experience of aging that those we loved have gone or are far from us; more and more the life of the aging is circumscribed into a narrow domain.

There is a moving image of this aspect of the life of the aging by the American poet E. A. Robinson. In his poem "Mr. Flood's Party," Robinson describes the celebration of sorts that old Eben Flood enjoys alone, up on a hillside, looking down on the places that he knew and loved and enjoyed with others when he was young.

> Alone, as if enduring to the end
> A valiant amor of scarred hopes ·outworn,
> He stood there in the middle of the road
> Like Roland's ghost winding a silent horn.
> Below him, in the town among the trees,
> Where friends of other days had honored him,
> A phantom salutation of the dead
> Rang thinly till old Eben's eyes were dim.
> . . . .
> There was not much that was ahead of him,
> And there was nothing in the town below—
> Where strangers would have shut the many doors
> That many friends had opened long ago.

In these words is captured the essence of being old: doors are closed that were opened long ago.

The old are perhaps the greatest and maybe in some ways the most miserable of all the minorities that our society discriminates against. Like blacks, women, and the young, they

Identity Crisis

have very little say, comparatively speaking, in the determination of the course of their lives. Like so many of these others also, they are encapsulated, shut off among their own, as though they have nothing to give that is wanted by others. Fundamentally, the problem for the aging is an *identity crisis.* It is the problem constituted by trying to determine who I am, and what my role is in relationship to the people around me. The aging are objects of great hostility as tyrants, and objects of great rejection as cantankerous, as though a man could be anything but cantankerous if his life is nothing but a series of rejections.

The aging are always and everywhere responded to as a burden. In our society, instead of facing up to this problem, we handle it as we do many of our problems: we pretend it does not exist. We gloss over aging and devote a considerable proportion of our national resources to perpetuate a deception which truly deceives no one, the lie that we are all eternally young.

As Hamlet said, holding in his hands the skull, "To this favour we must all come." The reality of our lives is that as time goes on, we grow older, and if we cannot find meaning and value in our later years, I think we betray the circumstance that our earlier years were also empty.

Maturation

Age is not only a loss of human powers, it is also in very significant degree the *maturation* and *fulfillment* of our powers. The poets have spoken very eloquently to this effect. In a poem called "Rabbi Ben Ezra," Robert Browning writes:

> Grow old along with me!
> The best is yet to be,
> The last of life, for which the first was made:
> . . . .

> Youth ended, I shall try
> My gain or loss thereby;
> Leave the fire ashes, what survives is gold:

There is a way, I think, in which all of us know that what survives is gold.

There are many dimensions of human experience in which the passage of time serves as a touchstone by which we distinguish between what only seems to be of value and what truly has worth. In the opening scenes of Oliver Goldsmith's play, *She Stoops to Conquer,* Hardcastle says to his wife Dorothy, "I love everything that's old: old friends, old times, old manners, old books, old wine; and I believe, Dorothy, you'll own, I have been pretty fond of an old wife." Aging not only gives the kind of quality that only old books, old wine, old friends can give; aging also brings with it a kind of wisdom to which the young cannot pretend without betraying their youth, and which we cannot ascribe to the young without betraying a groundless envy of their condition. For age carries with it a kind of perspective. A man can look back on the whole course of his life and the more he sees of his past, the more clearly, it seems to me, he can discern the outlines of his future, and the more profoundly, I believe, he can understand and appreciate the significance of his life.

I believe it is this fact that is responsible for the eccentricity that we so often associate with age. If the old are eccentric, it is because, as is often said, they march to the sound of a different drummer, as do the young also. This is only one of the many ways in which, it seems to me, the problems of aging are identical today with the problems of maturation, the problems of the young. Longfellow writes:

For age is opportunity no less
Than youth itself, though in another dress,
And as the evening twilight fades away
The sky is filled with stars invisible by day.

Those who are aging see the stars which to others are not yet in the sky. The aging enjoy therefore a kind of freedom to which we all aspire and which all who do not share it should envy. They are free of that daily round of events which seem in a limited perspective to be of such overriding importance but which the older among us can put in their proper place.

When Socrates was brought to trial for corrupting the young and was condemned to death, even those who condemned him were rather appalled at what they had done. They connived in a plan of escape for him, but Socrates wanted no part in it because, said he, I have lived my whole life in dedication to the principles of justice and truth, and shall I now in the short time remaining to me destroy the significance of all that has gone before? In many ways, it is the old that are to be envied by the young; they have so much less to lose that often they are capable of much more dedication and commitment to the values, ideals, and principles which provide meaning to all our lives.

Aging is not a problem peculiar to our time and place. But it may be that this problem is more pressing for us today because our development of medicine and related services is producing more and more a society of the aging. In the face of this problem it would seem to me that there are a few basic principles which are so clear and compelling as virtually to defy controversy.

Integration

First, we must truly practice *integration* with regard to the aging members of our population. Instead of isolating the older elements of society, instead of shutting them off, we must establish, not societies of senior citizens, so-called, but genuine communities in which the old, the middle aged, youth, and children are living together in the full richness of human experience. The old need, as we all need, to be needed. They need an opportunity to give love. They need an opportunity to be with all those other human beings who make life significant for any of us. Especially do the old need the recognition of the right to be heard, the right to share in the decisions which affect not only their own lives, but also the lives of all the other members of our society.

Second, the old need an opportunity for *productivity*. Our concept that a man has a useful life span of just so many years, and that on his sixtieth birthday, or sixty-second, or sixty-fifth, or whatever it may be, his productive capacity suddenly comes to an end, is a monstrous and inhuman concept. We must be flexible in our response to the gradually declining productivity of the aging, and recognize that there also comes with age a gradually *increasing* capacity to contribute to society.

Productivity

There is a beautiful and moving legend in the commentaries on the Bible. When Moses first came down from the mountain and saw the people worshiping the golden calf, he smashed the tablets of the Law, and afterwards ascended the mount once more and brought back two new tablets. According to the legend even the fragments of the broken tablets were kept in the Ark. For they also embodied a measure of holiness, and they also served as a guide and inspiration to the people.

The aging need opportunities for a continuation of the creative work which, fundamentally, is essential to any significant human experience. It is not enough to kill time with what are called hobbies, to sit about, even in the sunshine and even in the company of other aging, doing nothing more significant than waiting for death. The aging must be given opportunity to continue, as long as there is breath within them, to serve the people and purposes, the causes, institutions, and enterprises which gave meaning to the whole course of their lives. In particular, it seems to me important to provide occasions for the aging to work with the young. I do not know who gives more to whom when the old and the young spend time with one another. Surely that is an ideal pattern of human relations in which both parties to the relationship give so much and receive so much.

Growth

Perhaps most fundamental of all, more important than coping with the identity crisis, more important than being integrated into the community, more important even than continuing productivity, is continuing *growth*. A man grows so long as he is alive; when growth ends, life ends also. There's a wonderful story about Justice Oliver Wendell Holmes, who was in his nineties when President Franklin Delano Roosevelt was inaugurated. The President came to see the former Justice; he found Holmes sitting and reading, and said to him, "Mr. Justice, what are you reading?" Holmes replied, "Mr. President, I am reading the dialogues of Plato." President Roosevelt said to him, "And why, Mr. Justice, are you reading the dialogues of Plato?" The reply was, "Why, Mr. President, to improve my mind." When a man in his nineties reads Plato to improve his mind, he is still alive and, I believe, he shows what it means to be alive at any age: to be engaged continuously in the improvement of one's mind, in creative work, in relationship with other human beings, old and young, and in the giving of ourselves to a world that continues to give to us.

All this, I believe, was most eloquently expressed by Alfred Lord Tennyson, who himself lived to a ripe old age, in his poem, "Ulysses." There Tennyson depicted the closing years of the life of the great hero of the Homeric epics. His poem ends with these words:

> Old age hath yet his honor and his toil.
> Death closes all; but something ere the end,
> Some work of noble note, may yet be done,
> . . . .
> 'Tis not too late to seek a newer world.
> Push off, and sitting well in order smite
> The sounding furrows; for my purpose holds
> To sail beyond the sunset, and the baths
> Of all the western stars, until I die.
> . . . .
> Though much is taken, much abides; and though
> We are not now that strength which in old days
> Moved earth and heaven, that which we are, we are—
> One equal temper of heroic hearts,
> Made weak by time and fate, but strong in will
> To strive, to seek, to find, and not to yield.

On Death

For as long as there has been life, death has been the enemy. In our time medical technology has been making slow but steady progress in forestalling death. But whatever progress is made, to face death is the most universal and most inexorable of the demands that is made on us human beings.

Because of the advances in our technology, more and more human beings are dying of chronic diseases. This means that more people have time to face their own death and that more of us must cope with the sight of those we hold most dear slowly giving up their lives. Under these circumstances, more and more of the dying communicate to us a will to die. It is time for us to face squarely the responsibilities and the moral obligations that are involved in our considering whether there is such a thing as a *right* to die. Especially must we come to terms with the guilt that we all experience in the face of death—a guilt, it may be, because we feel ourselves burdened by the dying and wish it were over and done with, no matter how dearly we love them; and a guilt also, it may be, occasioned by the simple fact of survival: why should others die, and we remain alive, we who have done nothing to deserve the measureless gift of life?

All these problems are conditioned in our great Judeo-Christian tradition by a fundamental principle which we know as the principle of *the sanctity of life*. Life is sacred as the locus of all other values, and therefore as in itself the supreme value. But if we are quite honest with ourselves and with one another, we must acknowledge that in few areas of the domain of value is there more hypocrisy in our society than with regard to the sanctity of life. I mean more than the appalling rise in the number of individual acts of homicide, or even the mass murder in war. I mean also the many subtle ways in

Sanctity of Life

which what we profess to be the value that we place on life is not carried out in our actions. For instance, one need only consider the still shameful rate of infant mortality in the United States, the horrifying and steadily increasing rate of traffic fatalities, and the proliferation of many other more subtle patterns of destruction, both of ourselves, and of one another.

But we are hypocritical in another way as well. Though death is the enemy of life, we have contrived in our society to *glamorize* death, to paint it in the colors of life, indeed to make of it almost something more to be desired than life itself. Evelyn Waugh has written a brilliant and biting satire, called "The Loved One," of our patterns of denying and glossing over the bitter truths of death. I have sometimes thought that some of our beautiful cemeteries with their lawns and bronze and marble and music are trying to convey to us the message, "Don't grieve for the dead, they never had it so good."

If we were honest with ourselves and true to our own values, I think we would recognize that instead of glossing over the bitterness of death, what we should do is to intensify our awareness of it, and our recognition that death is an essential component of life. To be sure, the wise man, as Spinoza has counseled, thinks of life and not of death. Yet death remains a fact of life, and a very fundamental fact indeed.

The value that we place upon life and that we enshrine in the principle of the sanctity of life, like other absolutes, conceals qualifications and circumstances and conditions which are crucial for the actualization of the value in concrete **Quality of** situations. One must look, not to the mere continuation of **Life** life, but to the *quality* of the life that is being continued.

A man is injured; he has suffered severe brain damage; he

lies in a coma for hours, days, or even weeks. His life is perpetuated by the miracles of our medical technology. Yet he is no longer identifiably the person once known and loved, and it may well be that there is no prospect at all of his ever returning to that identity, or even so much as regaining consciousness. "As though to breathe were life," as the poet has it. There are deep human problems, I believe, which we must face and with which we will have to cope increasingly, in the moral principles that govern our perpetuation of life on a purely biological level, when what we know as something distinctively human is no longer present.

In medical practice, and in the tragic experience of many families, the problem of the dying becomes particularly acute when the death is a painful one. I cannot accept the doctrine one so often hears that there is something ennobling in suffering. I believe pain to be a degradation of the human spirit, as Job found pain to be not the instrument for recapturing his faith, but what almost cost him his faith, and with it all that made life worth living.

Dante, in his poetic vision of hell in the *Inferno,* describes it as a place where there is no longer even the hope of death; and alas, for some, death can be a hope. Nietzsche in the last century once very astutely remarked that the thought of suicide has saved many lives. The recognition, that is to say, that one can always die later, gives to man the courage to face up to the agonies which he may be experiencing for a time, and which may, in time, give way to the possibility of a continuing, meaningful, existence. But, if the agony does not give way, dying, the Roman Stoics were fond of saying, is also an act of life. How a man dies may be as much a measure of the man as how he lives. It may be, as some of the existentialists have urged in our time, that one of the greatest tasks of the living is to learn how to die.

Death means many different things to different people, as life has many different meanings. To die may be perceived as going home at last, or it may be seen as collapsing into nothingness. It may be experienced as a triumph, or it may be experienced as a defeat. There are those for whom the whole world comes to an end with their own existence, and others who are so deeply identified with their fellow human beings that their own death is only an incident in the ongoing of events that have meaning and value far beyond the boundaries of their own lives.

To die in a manner that is worthy of a human being is to die with a sense of one's identity as the human being that he is; as the locus of all the human values which intersect, which come to a meeting-point in his being, as an embodiment of human dignity. There are many in our time who have died the death of heroes, for there has been much inhumanity in our time. It is well to remember that even though the victims of inhumanity have been robbed of their lives, no one can rob a man of his humanity, of his soul, if he holds it fast. There was a document found in the rubble of the Warsaw ghetto after the revolt against the Nazis, who had been engaged in destroying it. The document recorded a meeting in which plans were weighed and decided upon for rising up in revolt. Death was on the agenda because life was no longer among the options open to those brave men and women. The choice that they did make was a choice between dying like the great human spirits they were, or allowing themselves to be reduced to the level of bestiality of those who were destroying them.

I think the great problem that we experience, a problem

known to every medical practitioner and known sooner or later to every human being who loves and loses a loved one, is the problem of how to deal with the dying. Often in the presence of death, we the living are dehumanized, because we dehumanize the dying. Precisely when they stand in greatest need of human closeness and warmth, our own fears and our own guilts turn us away from them. We even imagine that we can continue to deceive them about their own condition. Perhaps sometimes it is an act of kindness to conceal the truth from the dying. But it may also be that it is an act of cowardice. It may be that a man has a right to know when his life is drawing to a close, and a right also to share with us the knowledge of those last hours of his, so that he can die at peace with himself and with others, not isolated and abandoned precisely by those who mean the most to him. As the American poetess Emily Dickinson wrote, "Parting is all we know of heaven, and all we need of hell." I believe that we must recognize another principle, coordinate with the principle of the sanctity of life. That is the principle of the *acceptance* of death. This certainly does not mean giving up, surrendering to the enemy, or betraying the values for which life is the precondition. It simply means recognizing death as the inevitable accompaniment and culmination of life.

Acceptance

When Job is able to declare, "God gave, and God has taken away. Blessed be the name of God," he has come to an acceptance of the ills that flesh is heir to, and is able to experience life as a blessing, even with those ills.

There is a legend of a great sage who had two sons whom he loved dearly. On a day when he was away from home, suddenly his two sons died within the same hour. His wife tenderly laid them out in another room and covered them. When her husband returned, she said to him, "Many years ago a stranger passed this way, and left in my keeping two precious jewels. He was gone so long that I felt those jewels were my own. Today, unexpectedly, he reappeared and demanded that I return to him what is his. Must I, indeed, give them up?" He said to her, "How can you doubt where the course of virtue lies?" She took him by the hand to the other room, threw back the sheet, and said, "There lie the jewels." There must surely come a time for all of us when the jewels in our keeping are no longer present to us. Only, nothing is more characteristically human than for us to feel "Not yet! now is not the time!"

I think it is true that the acceptance of death depends upon its being a death in good time. It is in good time when it is in the fullness of years, and the fullness of years is not to be measured only in their number, but in the fullness of the days, and of the hours, in the fulfillments that were experienced. So long as a man can feel that each year of his life is the best, that each day is better than all the days that have gone before, that in this hour he knows the joy as well as the pain and the burden of being human, his life is being fulfilled. I suppose that a man finds it difficult, or even impossible, to accept death if till then he has not accepted life, if life has not accepted him.

There is a story in Scripture of the prophet Balaam, who was called upon to curse the Israelites, and who instead could only bless them, even expressing for himself the hope, "May I die the death of the righteous; may my end be like their end." He looked down upon their encampment and said, "How beautiful are your tents, O Jacob, how goodly your tabernacles." To be able to look upon human habitations and to see them as beautiful even though the tents will be folded and the people will pass, is to live, it seems to me, the life of the righteous, and to be able then to die, to come to an end, as the righteous do.

I do not believe that a whole life can be summed up in some memorable last words, but the Psalmist was able to put into as few words, and as memorable words as any, what it means to be able to experience both the sanctity of life and the acceptance of death, when he wrote, "My cup runneth over."

With this we come to the end of the last of our series. In these closing moments there rise to my mind the words which come after that line in the Psalms. They are: "May goodness and mercy follow all the days of my life." May they follow all *your* days, as I trust they will follow mine.

ACKNOWLEDGMENTS

The photographs on the pages indicated below are from the following sources:
CONGRAT-BUTLAR, pp. xii, 84
Stuart Abbey, pp. 10 (Photo by Abbey © 1973), 20, 28, 38 (Photo by Abbey © 1972), 66, 92
University of Michigan Information Services, p. 48